A History of Bahrain

Willem Meijer

Table of Contents

- **Introduction**

- **Chapter 1** The Land of Immortality: Dilmun and the Dawn of Civilization

- **Chapter 2** Under Hellenistic Influence: The Era of Tylos

- **Chapter 3** Between Empires: Persian Domination and the Rise of Nestorianism

- **Chapter 4** The Arrival of Islam and the Early Caliphates

- **Chapter 5** The Qarmatian Republic: A Challenge to Abbasid Authority

- **Chapter 6** The Age of Local Dynasties: Uyunids, Usfurids, and Jarwanids

- **Chapter 7** The Portuguese Era: A Century of European Control

- **Chapter 8** Persian and Omani Contests for the Islands

- **Chapter 9** The Rise of the Al Khalifa

- **Chapter 10** Pax Britannica: Treaties, Maritime Security, and British Influence

- **Chapter 11** The Pearl Industry: Boom, Bust, and Social Change

- **Chapter 12** Black Gold: The Discovery of Oil and the Transformation of a Nation

- **Chapter 13** The Winds of Change: Nationalism and the Path to Independence

- **Chapter 14** Building a Modern State: The Early Years of Independence (1971-1981)

- **Chapter 15** Navigating Regional Conflicts: The Iran-Iraq War and Gulf Tensions

- **Chapter 16** The 1990s Uprising: Demands for Political Reform

- **Chapter 17** A New Century, A New Charter: The National Action Charter of 2001

- **Chapter 18** Beyond the Oil Fields: Economic Diversification and Finance

- **Chapter 19** The Tumult of 2011: The Pearl Roundabout Protests

- **Chapter 20** A Decade of Reckoning: The Aftermath of the Uprising

- **Chapter 21** Bahrain on the World Stage: Foreign Policy in the 21st Century

- **Chapter 22** The Evolution of Bahraini Society: Culture, Identity, and Modernization

- **Chapter 23** The Changing Role of Women in Bahrain

- **Chapter 24** Crafting the Future: Bahrain's Economic Vision 2030

- **Chapter 25** Contemporary Challenges and the Road Ahead

- **Afterword**

Introduction

To write a history of an island is to tell a story of connection and isolation. Islands are worlds unto themselves, yet they are also magnets for the outside world, serving as ports, prizes, and strategic footholds. Few places on Earth embody this paradox more completely than the archipelago of Bahrain. For more than five millennia, this small cluster of islands in the Persian Gulf has been a pivotal center of trade, culture, and power, its destiny shaped as much by the ambitions of distant empires as by the resilience of its own people. Its story is one of remarkable continuity and startling transformation, a history written in the layers of ancient settlements, the shimmer of pearls, the glint of black gold, and the gleam of modern finance.

The very name "Bahrain" hints at the islands' unique character. In Arabic, *al-Bahrayn* is the dual form of *bahr*, meaning "sea," thus translating to "the Two Seas." The exact reference of this name is a subject of friendly debate. It may refer to the waters to the east and west of the main island, or perhaps the seas to its north and south. A more poetic and telling explanation points to the rare natural phenomenon where freshwater springs bubble up from aquifers deep beneath the seabed, creating a "sea" of fresh water within the salty sea of the Gulf. This unusual combination of freshwater abundance and strategic location made Bahrain an oasis and a sanctuary for mariners and traders from the dawn of civilization. It was a place where civilizations could meet, mingle, and trade goods and ideas.

The earliest chapters of Bahrain's story are shrouded in the mists of deep time, belonging to the civilization of Dilmun. For the ancient Sumerians of Mesopotamia, Dilmun was a sacred, almost mythical land, a commercial partner, and the fabled abode of the immortals. First mentioned in cuneiform tablets from the third millennium BC, Dilmun was a prosperous trading center that linked the great civilizations of Mesopotamia and the Indus Valley. The thousands of burial mounds that dot the Bahraini landscape, the largest prehistoric cemetery in the world, stand as silent testament to a sophisticated and populous society that flourished here for centuries. These ancient mounds and the excavated remains of Dilmun's capital at Qal'at al-Bahrain offer a tangible connection to a past where Bahrain was a vital node in the ancient world's global economy.

As the power of Dilmun waned, the islands did not fade into obscurity. Their strategic value ensured they would remain a coveted prize. During the Hellenistic period, after the conquests of Alexander the Great, Bahrain became known to the Greeks as Tylos. Serving as a center for the lucrative pearl trade, Tylos became part of a wider, Hellenized world, absorbing Greek cultural influences while retaining its unique Semitic character. This era marked the beginning of a long pattern in Bahraini history: the layering of foreign influence upon a resilient local foundation. Over the subsequent centuries, the islands fell under the sway of a succession of regional powers, including Persian dynasties like the Parthians and Sassanids, who recognized Bahrain's importance in controlling the vital trade routes of the Persian Gulf.

The arrival of Islam in the 7th century marked a profound turning point, integrating the islands firmly into the Arab and Islamic world. Yet, Bahrain's history continued to be punctuated by periods of fierce independence and external contest. The archipelago would host the radical Qarmatian republic, a fascinating and rebellious chapter that challenged the authority of the Abbasid Caliphate. It would later endure the ambitions of European colonial powers, most notably the Portuguese, who seized control of the islands in the 16th century as part of their quest to dominate the Indian Ocean trade routes. This was followed by renewed contests for influence between the Persians and Omanis, each vying for control of this strategic maritime hub.

The modern history of Bahrain begins with the rise of the Al Khalifa family, who arrived from the Arabian mainland and established their rule in 1783. Their arrival marks the genesis of the modern state. The subsequent era was defined by another, more formidable, foreign power: Great Britain. Seeking to secure its maritime routes to India and suppress piracy, Britain entered into a series of treaties with Bahrain's rulers beginning in the 19th century. These agreements culminated in Bahrain becoming a British protectorate, a status that would shape its political development for over a century. Britain managed Bahrain's defense and foreign affairs, a long and complex relationship that provided security but also entrenched British influence deep into the fabric of the state.

Throughout much of this period, and for centuries prior, Bahrain's economy was driven by a single, iridescent treasure: the natural pearl. For millennia, the oyster beds surrounding the islands produced some of the world's most sought-after pearls, creating a single-product economy that brought immense wealth but also great hardship. The grueling and perilous work of the pearl divers, the complex social structure it created, and the global trade it fueled defined life on the islands. Jewelers from Paris and merchants from Bombay flocked to Bahrain, making it the undisputed center of the global pearl trade. The collapse of this industry in the early 20th century, brought on by the advent of Japanese cultured pearls, could have spelled disaster. Instead, it coincided with a discovery that would transform Bahrain, and the entire region, forever.

In 1932, Bahrain became the first state on the Arab side of the Gulf to discover oil. The discovery ushered in an era of unprecedented change, fundamentally reshaping every aspect of Bahraini society. Oil revenue funded the development of a modern state, with new infrastructure, schools, and healthcare. It created new industries, such as refining and aluminum smelting, and attracted a large expatriate workforce, adding to the islands' cosmopolitan character. But this newfound wealth also brought new complexities, altering traditional social structures and creating new political and economic pressures. As the first Gulf nation to find oil, Bahrain would also be among the first to confront the challenges of a post-oil future, leading the way in efforts to diversify its economy.

The latter half of the 20th century was a period of profound political evolution. The currents of Arab nationalism, combined with Britain's decision to withdraw its forces from the Gulf, set Bahrain on the path to sovereignty. On August 15, 1971, Bahrain declared its independence, taking its place on the world stage as a sovereign nation. The decades that followed were dedicated to the complex task of state-building, navigating regional conflicts, and balancing tradition with modernity. This journey has not been without its challenges. The nation has experienced periods of political unrest, most notably the uprising in the 1990s and the large-scale protests of 2011, which reflected deep-seated demands for political reform and greater social equity.

In the new millennium, Bahrain has embarked on ambitious reforms. The National Action Charter of 2001, approved by a massive public referendum, transformed the country into a constitutional monarchy and was hailed as the start of a new era of political openness. This commitment to reform has been paired with a forward-looking economic strategy. Recognizing the limitations of its oil reserves, Bahrain has worked to position itself as a leading financial hub and a diversified, globally competitive economy, guided by its Economic Vision 2030.

This book traces the long and multifaceted history of this remarkable archipelago. It is a story that stretches from the sacred land of Dilmun to the modern financial district of Manama. It is a history of a people whose fortunes have been tied to the sea, first through the bounty of its pearls and later through the wealth that lay beneath it. It is the story of a nation at the crossroads of empires, a place of constant interaction between local identity and foreign influence. From the age of sail to the age of oil and beyond, Bahrain's history is a compelling testament to the power of adaptation, resilience, and a unique geographical destiny.

CHAPTER ONE: The Land of Immortality: Dilmun and the Dawn of Civilization

Before there were written histories, there were myths. In the clay tablets of ancient Sumer, unearthed from the sands of modern Iraq, scribes wrote of a land beyond the southern horizon—a pure, bright, and sacred place where the sun rose. This was Dilmun, a veritable paradise where disease and death were unknown, where predators did not kill, and the raven did not caw. It was to Dilmun that the gods brought the hero of the great flood, Utnapishtim, to live forever as an immortal. And it was in this blessed land that the great hero Gilgamesh, tormented by the death of his friend Enkidu, traveled in his desperate search for the secret of eternal life. For centuries, Dilmun was a name whispered in myth, a semi-divine place located somewhere in the lower sea, the ancient name for the Persian Gulf. Scholars debated its location, but its physical existence remained as ethereal as the stories told about it. It was not until the shovels of modern archaeology bit into the soil of Bahrain in the mid-20th century that the lost land of Dilmun was finally found.

The Danish archaeological teams who began systematic excavations in the 1950s uncovered something extraordinary. Beneath a formidable 16th-century Portuguese fort lay the ruins of a sprawling ancient city. Layer upon layer of human occupation, stretching back to roughly 2300 BC, formed an artificial hill, or tell—the remains of what was once the capital of Dilmun. This site, now known as Qal'at al-Bahrain and recognized as a UNESCO World Heritage Site, confirmed Bahrain as the heart of the long-lost civilization. The evidence was unmistakable: here was a powerful and prosperous society that flourished during the Bronze Age, perfectly positioned to become a pivotal link between the great civilizations of Mesopotamia to the north and the Indus Valley to the east.

Dilmun was, above all, a nation of merchants. Its strategic location, combined with the rare abundance of fresh artesian water that gave Bahrain its name ("the Two Seas"), made it an indispensable port of call on the arduous maritime trade routes of the ancient world. Sumerian and Akkadian cuneiform texts do not just speak of Dilmun in mythological terms; they are also filled with commercial accounts. Inscriptions from kings like Ur-Nanshe of Lagash and Sargon of Akkad boast of ships from Dilmun arriving at their quays, laden with tribute and goods from distant lands. For the resource-hungry cities of Mesopotamia, built on alluvial plains with little wood, stone, or metal, Dilmun was the essential middleman. It was the gateway to the riches of the East.

The lynchpin of Dilmun's economy was copper. The metal, crucial for tools and weapons in the Bronze Age, was mined in the land of Magan, widely identified with modern- Oman, and then shipped to Dilmun for processing and re-export to the cities of Sumer. Archaeologists have unearthed the physical evidence of this vast trade network: copper ingots, workshops, and distinctive pottery. But the trade was far from a one-way street. In return for raw materials, Mesopotamian grain, textiles, and oils flowed south through Dilmun. From the Indus Valley, known to the Sumerians as Meluhha, came luxury goods: carnelian beads, ivory, and exotic woods. Dilmun was the central hub in this international system, a bustling entrepôt where goods were exchanged, weighed, and recorded. Its prosperity, which peaked between 2050 and 1750 BC, was built not on conquest, but on commerce.

This sophisticated trading network required an equally sophisticated system of administration. The hallmark of Dilmunite commerce, and its most original artistic contribution, was the circular stamp seal. While Mesopotamian merchants used cylindrical seals and the Indus Valley civilization favored square ones, Dilmun developed its own unique, circular design. These small, exquisitely carved objects, typically made of steatite (soapstone), were more than just personal signatures. Pressed into clay, they authenticated documents, secured merchandise, and identified ownership. Each seal was a miniature masterpiece, depicting scenes from daily life, mythology, and nature—gazelles, bulls, palm trees, and human figures. Found in great numbers in Bahrain and as far afield as modern-day Kuwait and the

Mesopotamian city of Ur, these seals are tangible evidence of a complex and highly organized society. They also likely served a deeper purpose as protective amulets, invoking divine protection over the merchant and his goods, a vital reassurance on long and perilous journeys.

Dilmun's sacred reputation in Mesopotamian mythology was not just a literary flourish; it was intertwined with its physical reality and its religious practices. The Sumerian creation myth of Enki and Ninhursag is explicitly set in Dilmun. The story describes a pristine, virginal land that lacks only one thing: fresh water. The great god Enki, the lord of wisdom and sweet waters, commands the sun god Utu to fill the land with fresh water from the earth, transforming it into a divine garden. This myth powerfully echoes Bahrain's unique hydrogeology, where freshwater springs well up from underground aquifers, even from beneath the salty seabed. The myth legitimized Dilmun's special status; its very fertility was a gift from the gods.

This veneration of fresh water is given monumental form at the Barbar Temple complex, another of Bahrain's key archaeological sites. Dating back to around 3000 BC, the site consists of three temples built successively on top of one another, each centered around a sacred well. The well-preserved limestone altars and basins suggest that rituals involving water purification were central to the religious life of the Dilmunites. The temple was likely dedicated to Enki himself, a belief reinforced by the discovery of a magnificent copper bull's head, an animal often associated with fertility and divine power in the ancient Near East. The Barbar Temple, along with evidence of snake cults found in some burial sites, provides a window into a belief system that, while influenced by Mesopotamia, retained its own unique local character.

Perhaps the most astonishing and visible legacy of the Dilmun civilization is the vast necropolis that covers the northern part of the island. Tens of thousands of burial mounds, ranging from small, simple tumuli to towering "royal" tombs, create a unique, undulating landscape. These mounds, which together form the largest prehistoric cemetery in the world, stand as a silent testament to a large and prosperous population that believed deeply in an afterlife. Built between approximately 2200 and 1750 BC, the mounds were constructed as cylindrical stone towers which, over millennia, have weathered into their current dome-like shape.

The sheer number and density of the graves are staggering. Early estimates suggested as many as 170,000 mounds, though the number of well-preserved examples is now closer to 11,000. Their construction reflects a clear social hierarchy. The majority are the graves of ordinary people, relatively small and containing a single stone-lined chamber. The deceased were typically laid on their right side, accompanied by a few personal items like pottery, a seal, or some jewelry for their journey to the next world. Dominating the landscape in the village of A'ali, however, are the so-called royal mounds. These are massive, two-storied sepulchral towers, some reaching up to 15 meters in height and 45 meters in diameter, built for the ruling elite of Dilmun. Though most were looted in antiquity, the scale of these tombs demonstrates the power and wealth concentrated in the hands of a few. The burial mounds, in their entirety, reveal a society that invested enormous collective effort in honoring its dead, from the commoner to the king.

Life in Dilmun was sustained by more than just trade. The same freshwater that gave the islands their sacred status also supported a thriving agricultural economy. Date palms, which grew in abundance, were a staple of the diet and a key export. The seas provided fish and, of course, the pearls that would bring the islands renewed fame in later centuries. At the remarkable settlement site near the modern village of Saar, archaeologists have uncovered an entire, well-preserved Dilmunite town. Dating to the early second millennium BC, the town provides an intimate glimpse into the daily lives of its inhabitants. Houses, built to a uniform plan, cluster around a main street and a temple. Ovens, storage rooms, and even what appear to be shops have been identified, painting a picture of a well-organized urban community.

The civilization of Dilmun was not static. It existed for well over two millennia, experiencing periods of growth, consolidation, and decline. After its golden age in the early second millennium BC, Dilmun's fortunes became increasingly tied to the shifting powers in Mesopotamia. For a time, it fell under the control of the Kassite dynasty of Babylon, and later inscriptions show Assyrian kings claiming sovereignty over the island. The rise of piracy in the Gulf after 1000 BC appears to have severely disrupted the old trade routes, weakening Dilmun's commercial dominance. By the 6th century BC, Dilmun was incorporated into the Neo-Babylonian Empire, and after the fall of Babylon in 538 BC, the name itself gradually faded from use. The land of immortality, the vital hub of the Bronze Age world, was entering a new phase of its history, one in which it would be known by another name.

CHAPTER TWO: Under Hellenistic Influence: The Era of Tylos

The final centuries of the first millennium BC saw a new wind blow from the West, carrying with it soldiers, merchants, and ideas that would once again reshape the fortunes of Bahrain. The old name, Dilmun, freighted with millennia of history and myth, had faded into obscurity. The island had become a relatively quiet backwater within the vast Achaemenid Persian Empire. Then, in a whirlwind campaign that redrew the map of the known world, the armies of Alexander the Great swept across Persia, shattering an empire and inaugurating a new era. Suddenly, the island found itself on the edge of a new, Greek-speaking world, a world with an insatiable curiosity and a keen eye for commerce.

For the Greeks, the Persian Gulf was a mysterious and largely uncharted body of water. Alexander, ever the ambitious strategist and explorer, intended to change that. As his land campaign wound down in India, he dispatched a fleet under the command of his trusted admiral, Nearchus, on a perilous voyage of discovery. The mission, which began in 325 BC, was to explore the coastline from the mouth of the Indus River back to the head of the Gulf. It was during this pioneering expedition that Greek ships, for the first time in recorded history, dropped anchor off Bahrain's shores.

Nearchus and his men found a verdant, thriving island. His scribes, likely drawing on local pronunciations of the old name "Dilmun" or "Tilmun," Hellenized it into "Tylos." And so, Bahrain was reborn on the maps and in the literature of the classical West. Nearchus's reports described a prosperous commercial center, noting its large plantations of cotton trees used to manufacture fine textiles called *sindones*, which were traded as far as Arabia. The Greek historian Theophrastus, relaying information from another of Alexander's explorers, Androsthenes of Thasos, added that Tylos was also known for exporting high-quality walking canes, which were apparently in vogue among the fashionable set in Babylon. The arrival of Nearchus was more than a fleeting visit; it marked the formal inclusion of the island into the Hellenistic world.

Following Alexander's untimely death in 323 BC, his enormous empire was fractured among his generals. The vast eastern territories, including Mesopotamia and the Persian Gulf, fell to his general Seleucus I Nicator, who founded the Seleucid Empire. For the next century and a half, Tylos existed under the tutelage of this powerful Hellenistic state. While it remains uncertain whether the island was a directly administered province or a largely autonomous vassal, the archaeological evidence at Qal'at al-Bahrain suggests it may have served as a Seleucid base in the Gulf. Whatever its precise political status, Tylos flourished during this period. It was a port of call for the Greek military fleet and, more importantly, it regained its role as a vibrant hub of international trade, connecting the Mediterranean world with the markets of the East.

The primary engine of Tylos's prosperity was a treasure that had long been harvested from its surrounding waters but was now in unprecedented demand: the pearl. While the pearl fisheries had been known since antiquity, the wealth and luxury of the Hellenistic kingdoms and, later, the Roman Empire, created a voracious new market. Roman historian Pliny the Elder, writing in the 1st century AD, devoted considerable attention to the pearls of Tylos, calling them the most highly prized in the world. He declared that "the first place therefore and the topmost rank among all things of price is held by pearls." He noted that Tylos was "famous for the vast number of its pearls" and that Roman luxury had even given them the name *uniones*, or "unique gems," because no two were ever exactly alike.

Pliny's account, filled with a mixture of fact and poetic fancy, described how the oysters were believed to be impregnated by dewdrops from the heavens, with the quality of the pearl depending on the purity of the dew. He wrote of the perilous work of the divers, who had to contend with sharks—"sea-dogs," as he called them—to retrieve the precious shells from the seabed. So great was the Roman demand for these symbols of wealth and status that fortunes were spent on them. Bahrain's pearls adorned the ears and fingers of the Roman elite, solidifying the island's reputation across the known world as the preeminent source of this marine jewel.

This economic boom was accompanied by a significant cultural shift. While the underlying Semitic culture remained strong, with Aramaic serving as the common language, a veneer of Hellenism spread across the island, particularly among the upper classes. Greek became a language of administration and commerce, Greek athletic contests were held, and local coinage was struck showing a seated Zeus, who may have been a syncretized form of the Arabian sun-god, Shams. Greek inscriptions discovered in Bahrain provide tangible proof of the deep cultural interaction between the islanders and the Hellenistic world. Imported goods from across the Greek world, including fine pottery, glassware, and alabaster containers, became common, attesting to the island's renewed and complex trade network.

The most striking evidence of this cultural fusion comes from the island's cemeteries. The ancient Dilmunite tradition of constructing burial mounds did not disappear, but it was transformed. The Tylos-era necropolises, found in areas like Shakhura and Abu Saiba, consist of numerous individual graves, often clustered together and sometimes superimposed, which over centuries merged to form large, irregular hillocks. These burial sites, densely packed with hundreds of graves, show that the northern part of the island was heavily populated during this period. Though many tombs were plundered in antiquity, those that remain have yielded a wealth of artifacts.

Inside these graves, archaeologists have found a fascinating blend of local tradition and Hellenistic innovation. The deceased were often buried with a rich collection of goods for the afterlife, including glazed pottery, glass vessels, and fine jewelry. Most remarkable, however, are the funerary stelae, or gravestones. Carved from local limestone, these stelae bear portraits of the deceased. The style is a unique synthesis of Greek artistic conventions and local Semitic features. The figures are often depicted in a stiff, frontal pose, but their clothing, hairstyles, and the execution of their facial features show clear Hellenistic influence. One poignant example, dubbed the "little girl tombstone," captures the solemn face of a child, a powerful and personal link to the people who inhabited Tylos two millennia ago. These gravestones represent a distinct local school of art, a testament to how the people of Tylos adopted and adapted foreign styles to fit their own cultural context.

By the middle of the second century BC, the power of the Seleucid Empire began to wane. Internal strife and pressure from the rising power of Parthia in Persia and Rome in the west weakened its grip on its eastern territories. This power vacuum at the head of the Gulf allowed for the emergence of a new regional player: the kingdom of Characene. Founded around 129 BC by a former Seleucid governor named Hyspaosines, Characene was centered on the port city of Charax Spasinou (in modern-day Kuwait). As a commercially savvy state that controlled the lucrative trade routes into Mesopotamia, Characene quickly extended its influence south, and Tylos fell under its sway.

Direct evidence of Characene's control comes from a Greek inscription discovered in Bahrain. It records the dedication of a temple to the twin gods Castor and Pollux (the Dioscuri) by a military governor named Kephisodoros, acting in the name of King Hyspaosines and his wife, Queen Thalassia. This inscription confirms that Hyspaosines appointed a *strategos*, or military governor, to rule over "Tylos and the Islands," the official name for the archipelago. For the next few centuries, Tylos would remain linked to Characene, which itself was usually a vassal of the powerful Parthian Empire. Another inscription from the Syrian city of Palmyra mentions a man named Meredates, a member of the Parthian royal family and king of Characene, who appointed a satrap to govern Tylos around 131 AD.

Under Characene and Parthian suzerainty, Tylos continued its role as a prosperous trading center. The pearl trade remained the bedrock of its economy, and its strategic position ensured it remained a key node in the maritime routes that connected the

Roman Empire with Persia, India, and beyond. This period represented not a sharp break from the Seleucid era, but rather a continuation of the island's Hellenistic character under new political masters. The cultural fusion that had begun with Nearchus's arrival deepened, creating a unique Tylos culture that was at once cosmopolitan and distinctly Bahraini. The island was a meeting point of civilizations—Greek, Persian, Mesopotamian, and Arabian—a role it was destined to play many times over in its long history.

CHAPTER THREE: Between Empires: Persian Domination and the Rise of Nestorianism

As the Hellenistic star of the Seleucids waned, a new and formidable power arose to the east. The Parthians, and then more decisively, the Sassanids, re-established Persian imperial might, casting a long shadow over Mesopotamia and the Persian Gulf. For Bahrain, the era of Tylos, with its unique fusion of Greek and Semitic culture, gave way to a long period under the direct gaze of a Zoroastrian empire. This was not a radical break with the past so much as a change of management. The islands' strategic and commercial importance remained undiminished, but their political and cultural orientation shifted decisively toward the Persian mainland. Over the course of four centuries, Bahrain would be integrated into the Sassanian world, a process that saw it become not only a key administrative outpost but also, rather unexpectedly, a vibrant and influential center of Christianity.

The transition began in earnest in the 3rd century AD with the arrival of a new, ambitious dynasty in Persia. Ardashir I, a local ruler from the province of Persis, overthrew the last Parthian king in 224 AD and founded the Sassanian Empire. Unlike the more decentralized Parthians, the Sassanians were aggressive centralizers, determined to secure every border of their new domain, which they called *Eranshahr*, the "Realm of the Iranians." Ardashir, known as "the Unifier," quickly turned his attention to the vital trade routes of the Persian Gulf. He marched his armies down the coast, subjugating Oman and Bahrain and defeating the local ruler, a figure named Sanatruq, who was likely a Parthian-appointed governor. For the Sassanians, control of the Gulf was not optional; it was essential for dominating the sea lanes to India and for securing their southern flank against Roman influence and roaming Arab tribes.

To solidify his control, Ardashir appointed his son, the future emperor Shapur I, as the first Sassanian governor of the region. This act signaled the islands' importance. Bahrain was not merely a vassal but an integral part of the imperial structure. Administratively, the archipelago became a district known as Mishmahig. This district was part of a larger southern province that encompassed the entire western coast of the Gulf. The other districts in this province were Haggar (centered on modern Hofuf) and Batan Ardashir (centered on modern Al-Qatif). The name Mishmahig is thought to be Middle Persian for "ewe-fish," perhaps a strange but evocative name for an island famed for its marine resources. Shapur is even said to have founded a new city on the island, naming it Batan Ardashir in honor of his father, though its precise location has been lost to time.

Life under the Sassanians involved a delicate balance. A Persian ruling class and military garrisons were established, and Zoroastrianism was the state religion. Middle Persian, or Pahlavi, became the language of administration. Yet, the majority of the population remained ethnically Arab, and the common tongue was Aramaic, the lingua franca of the region for centuries. The economy continued to turn on the familiar axes of date palm cultivation, fishing, and, above all, the pearl trade. The Sassanians, themselves shrewd merchants, were content to oversee and tax this lucrative commerce rather than upend it. The islands thus became a multicultural society, a mosaic of Arab tribesmen, Persian administrators, Aramaic-speaking townsfolk, and a small Jewish community, all living under the authority of the Sassanian *shahanshah*, the King of Kings.

This complex society provided fertile ground for a new religious movement that was quietly spreading eastward from the Roman Empire. Christianity had arrived in Mesopotamia at an early date, and by the Sassanian period, it had a robust and organized presence. However, this was not the Christianity of Rome or Constantinople. This was the Church of the East, a distinct branch of the faith that used Syriac, a dialect of Aramaic, as its liturgical language. Its followers would later be labeled "Nestorians" by their Western counterparts due to a theological dispute over the nature of Christ, a label they did not use themselves.

The relationship between the Sassanian state and its Christian subjects was often fraught with suspicion. As Christianity became the state religion of the rival Roman (and later Byzantine) Empire, Sassanian rulers frequently viewed their own Christian populations as a potential fifth column, leading to periods of brutal persecution. However, the Church of the East's theological separation from the Byzantine church provided it with a degree of political cover. By establishing its own distinct identity, it could more convincingly argue its loyalty to the Persian throne. For many Christians fleeing Roman persecution, Sassanian territory, including its outposts in the Gulf, became a refuge.

The Persian Gulf, with its constant traffic of merchants, sailors, and migrants, acted as a natural conduit for the spread of the new faith. By the 5th century, Bahrain had emerged as a significant center for the Church of the East. The island became the seat of a bishop, a clear sign of a well-established and organized Christian community. This episcopal see was located in the village of Samaheej on the northern coast of Muharraq island. Ancient church records, known as the *Synodicon Orientale*, refer to the diocese by a Syriac version of the island's administrative name: Beth Qatraye, which often encompassed the Qatar peninsula as well.

These records provide tantalizing glimpses into the life of the early Bahraini church. They mention bishops from "Meshmahig" (a corruption of Samaheej) attending important church synods in the Sassanian capital of Seleucia-Ctesiphon. The relationship with the central church authorities was not always smooth. In 410 AD, a bishop from the island named Batai was excommunicated for unspecified reasons. More than two centuries later, in the mid-7th century, another bishop was condemned for challenging the authority of the Patriarch. These disputes, while problematic at the time, are invaluable for historians, as they confirm the existence of a confident, and at times defiant, Christian hierarchy in Bahrain that was an active participant in the wider affairs of the Church of the East.

Until recently, the evidence for this flourishing Christian past was almost entirely literary. Place names offered clues—the village of Al Dair, for instance, simply means "the monastery" in Arabic. But the physical proof remained elusive. This changed dramatically with recent archaeological excavations. In the village of Samaheej, under the ruins of a 17th-century mosque, a joint Bahraini-British team uncovered the foundations of a large, well-built complex. Radiocarbon dating confirmed that the building was occupied between the mid-4th and mid-8th centuries AD.

The substantial structure, measuring 17 by 10 meters, consists of several rooms, including a kitchen with built-in ovens, a dining room, and living quarters, all with plastered walls and floors. Its size and complexity suggest it was not an ordinary house but rather a public building of some importance, perhaps a monastery or even the official residence of the bishop of Meshmahig. The Christian identity of its inhabitants is unmistakable. Archaeologists found plaster crosses that once adorned the walls, another small cross that may have been a personal item, and graffiti scratched into the plaster depicting a fish and what appears to be a Chi-Rho—both potent early Christian symbols. The discovery of this site provides the first concrete archaeological evidence for Bahrain's pre-Islamic Christian community, transforming what was once known only from scattered texts into a tangible reality.

The community at Beth Qatraye was not just a remote outpost of the faithful; it developed into a significant center of intellectual and spiritual life for the entire Church of the East. In the 7th and 8th centuries, the region produced several notable Syriac-language writers and theologians. Figures such as Dadisho Qatraya, Gabriel of Qatar, and, most famously, Isaac of Nineveh (also known as Isaac the Syrian) were all born in Beth Qatraye. Their writings on monasticism and mysticism became profoundly influential and were translated into Greek, Arabic, and eventually Latin, impacting both Eastern and Western Christian thought for centuries to come. The emergence of such a vibrant literary and theological culture demonstrates that Christianity in Bahrain was deep-rooted, intellectually rigorous, and far from isolated.

Throughout the Sassanian period, Bahrain's fate was also intertwined with another major power in the region: the Lakhmids. Based in their capital of Al-Hira in southern Mesopotamia, the Lakhmids were an Arab dynasty that ruled a buffer kingdom as vassals of the Sassanian emperors. Their primary role was to manage the numerous Arab tribes of the peninsula and act as a check against the Ghassanids, a rival Arab kingdom allied with the Byzantines. The Sassanian emperor often delegated authority over the Arab tribes of the Gulf to the Lakhmid kings. At the height of their power in the 6th century, the Lakhmid ruler Mundhir III was made king over a vast swathe of Arabia, including Bahrain, by the emperor Khosrow I. This meant that for much of this era, Bahrain was subject to a dual layer of authority: direct Sassanian administration and the more immediate influence of their powerful Arab vassals.

By the early 7th century, the Sassanian Empire, which had dominated the region for four hundred years, was beginning to show signs of exhaustion. Decades of debilitating warfare with the Byzantine Empire had drained its treasury and manpower. In 602, in a disastrous miscalculation, the Sassanian emperor Khosrow II executed the last Lakhmid king, Nu'man III, and annexed his kingdom directly. This dismantled the buffer system that had kept the desert tribes in check for centuries, creating a power vacuum and alienating many Arabs who had been loyal to the Lakhmids. This internal turmoil left the empire's southern flank exposed. The Persian governor of Bahrain at this time was an Arab chief from the Tamim tribe named Al-Mundhir ibn Sawa Al-Tamimi. He ruled over a diverse populace of Arabs, Persians, Christians, Jews, and Zoroastrians. It was to this ruler, in this powerful but precarious Sassanian outpost, that a letter would arrive from the west in 628 AD, carrying a message that would once again set the islands on a profoundly new course.

CHAPTER FOUR: The Arrival of Islam and the Early Caliphates

In the year 628 AD, a messenger on a dusty camel arrived in the Sassanian province of Mishmahig, carrying a letter that would irrevocably alter the islands' destiny. The recipient was the Persian-appointed governor, Al-Mundhir ibn Sawa Al-Tamimi, an Arab chief who presided over a complex society of Arabs, Persians, Nestorian Christians, Jews, and Zoroastrians. The sender was a figure who, from the distant oasis town of Medina in the Hejaz, was beginning to reshape the political and spiritual landscape of Arabia: the Prophet Muhammad. The letter, carried by an envoy named Al-Ala Al-Hadrami, was concise and direct, an invitation to a new order and a new faith. It called on Al-Mundhir to abandon the old ways and embrace Islam.

Unlike the dismissive and contemptuous response the Prophet's letters received from the great emperors of Persia and Byzantium, Al-Mundhir's reaction was one of careful consideration. He consulted with representatives of the diverse communities under his rule. According to traditional accounts, he found his people, particularly the Arab tribes, receptive to the new message. In a reply to the Prophet, Al-Mundhir confirmed that while some had embraced Islam, others, particularly the Jewish and Magian (Zoroastrian) communities, wished to maintain their ancestral faiths. The Prophet's response was a landmark moment, setting a precedent for Islamic governance. He confirmed Al-Mundhir in his post, instructed that new Muslims be welcomed, and stipulated that Jews and Zoroastrians who did not convert would be protected upon payment of a poll tax known as the *jizya*.

This exchange marked a remarkably peaceful transition. There was no conquest, no great battle for Bahrain. Instead, its ruler and a significant portion of its people voluntarily entered the fold of Islam, transforming the islands from a Persian imperial outpost into a component of the nascent Muslim state. The powerful Abd al-Qays tribe, which dominated the region, was among the earliest and most enthusiastic converts. So swift was their adoption of the new faith that a mosque was established at Juwatha, in the nearby oasis of Al-Ahsa, which was part of the wider Bahrain region. This mosque is traditionally held to be the first site outside Medina where Friday congregational prayers were held. For the Christian communities of Samaheej and the Persian Zoroastrians, the change of authority brought a new reality. They were no longer subjects of a Zoroastrian king but a protected, tax-paying minority under Muslim rule, their fortunes now tied to the growing power in Medina.

The new order faced its first severe test just a few years later. The death of the Prophet Muhammad in 632 AD sent shockwaves across Arabia. With the unifying figure gone, many tribes who had pledged allegiance saw their pact as a personal one that had now lapsed. Across the peninsula, a series of rebellions known as the Ridda Wars erupted, challenging the authority of the Prophet's successor, the first Caliph, Abu Bakr. Bahrain was plunged into this turmoil. The passing of its own pro-Muslim governor, Al-Mundhir, at around the same time created a power vacuum. A faction from the Banu Bakr tribe, led by a descendant of the old Lakhmid kings, rose in rebellion, seeking to restore the old order and sever ties with Medina.

The rebels gained the upper hand, besieging the loyalist Abd al-Qays tribe, who had fortified themselves in the Juwatha oasis. The situation was dire. However, the Abd al-Qays held firm, a crucial act of loyalty that prevented the complete loss of eastern Arabia. In response, Caliph Abu Bakr dispatched a familiar face to the region: Al-Ala Al-Hadrami, the very same envoy who had first brought the message of Islam to Bahrain. Now returning as a military commander, Al-Ala's forces relieved the siege at Juwatha and confronted the main rebel army, which had entrenched itself in a fortress at Hajr. In a decisive engagement, Al-Ala mounted a surprise night attack, storming the fortress and routing the rebel army. The rebels fled towards the coast and the island of Darin, but they were pursued and decisively defeated. The Ridda Wars in Bahrain were over by early 633, and the authority of the Caliphate was firmly stamped upon the region.

With its loyalty proven in the crucible of the Ridda Wars, Bahrain became a fully integrated province of the Rashidun Caliphate, the empire of the first four "Rightly Guided" Caliphs who ruled from Medina. It ceased to be a frontier zone and became a functioning administrative and military district. Al-Ala Al-Hadrami remained as its governor for a time, overseeing the collection of taxes and the establishment of Islamic governance. Later, during the reign of the second Caliph, Umar I, other notable companions of the Prophet, such as Abu Hurayrah and Uthman ibn Abi Al Aas, served as governors of the islands. Bahrain's strategic location and maritime expertise were not lost on the new rulers. Under Caliph Umar, the governor Al-Ala, despite lacking explicit orders, used Bahrain as a base to launch the first Arab naval expedition against the Sassanian coast of Persia. Though the raid was ultimately censured by the famously cautious Caliph, who disliked sea campaigns, it was a clear harbinger of the future. Bahrain was no longer a recipient of imperial power from Persia; it was now a launching pad for the conquest of Persia itself.

The assassination of the fourth Caliph, Ali, in 661 and the subsequent rise of the Umayyad dynasty marked another significant shift. The capital of the Islamic empire moved from Medina to Damascus, a city far removed from the Persian Gulf. For Bahrain, this meant a return to being a relatively remote province, governed from afar. The Umayyads likely exerted their control indirectly, but the islands remained within their political orbit. One of the earliest mosques on the islands themselves, the Al Khamis Mosque, was founded during the reign of the Umayyad Caliph Umar II around 692 AD, a testament to the institutionalization of Islam in Bahraini society. Economically, life continued much as before. The pearl and date trades prospered, now oriented towards the great markets of the Caliphate, especially in Mesopotamia.

The Umayyad century, however, was also a period of profound political and religious ferment throughout the Islamic world. Opposition to what many saw as the worldly and dynastic rule of the Umayyads festered, giving rise to various dissident movements. In the deserts and oases of eastern Arabia, the most potent of these movements was that of the Kharijites. Emerging from the first great civil war in Islam, the Kharijites were religious puritans and radical egalitarians. They believed that any Muslim, regardless of lineage, could be Caliph, and that any ruler who deviated from the strict path of the Quran and the example of the Prophet was an apostate who must be overthrown. Their uncompromising zeal and militant opposition to the Damascus-based caliphate found fertile ground in the provinces.

During the Second Islamic Civil War, which erupted after the death of the first Umayyad Caliph's son, Yazid I, the central authority of Damascus weakened considerably. This power vacuum allowed Kharijite bands to operate with near impunity. One of the most successful Kharijite leaders was Najda ibn Amir al-Hanafi, from the Yamama region of central Arabia. Leading a faction that became known as the Najdat, he broke with the more extreme Kharijites and established his own state across much of eastern and central Arabia. Around 685, Najda's forces expanded into Bahrain, taking control of the islands and incorporating them into his short-lived Kharijite proto-caliphate. For a few years, Bahrain was ruled not from Damascus, but from the heart of Arabia by a rebel leader who defied both the Umayyads and their rivals. The Umayyad Caliph Abd al-Malik ibn Marwan, once he had consolidated his power elsewhere, dispatched an army to restore order. The Kharijite forces were defeated, their leader killed, and by 693, Bahrain was brought back under Umayyad control.

The year 750 marked a seismic shift in the Islamic world. The Abbasid Revolution, originating in the eastern province of Khurasan, swept across the empire, destroying the Umayyads and establishing a new caliphal dynasty. The Abbasids moved the capital from Damascus to a newly built city in Mesopotamia: Baghdad. This move had profound implications for Bahrain. Suddenly, the center of imperial power was once again just to the north, at the head of the Persian Gulf, much as it had been under the Babylonians and Sassanians. The trade routes through the Gulf surged with new importance as Baghdad became the commercial and intellectual center of the world. Bahrain, now often administered as part of a larger province including Yamama and Oman, prospered from this renewed focus on eastern trade.

Under powerful early Abbasid Caliphs like Abu Ja'far al-Mansur, central control was firmly re-established. In 768, after a local leader was killed, Al-Mansur sent an army led by Uqba bin Saleem to secure Bahrain, and its treasures were duly sent to Baghdad. For the next century, the islands remained a relatively quiet, if prosperous, part of the Abbasid empire. Intellectual life flourished, and Bahrain became known as a center for scholarship. However, the immense wealth and luxury of the Abbasid court in Baghdad stood in stark contrast to the realities of life in many of the provinces. As the 9th century progressed, the central authority of the Caliphs began to fray at the edges. In the salt flats of southern Iraq, not far from Bahrain, the massive and brutal Zanj Rebellion, a revolt of enslaved East Africans, raged for years, shaking the foundations of the empire. It was a sign of deep social and economic discontent. In the towns and oases of Bahrain, these same currents of dissent were beginning to flow, mingling with esoteric religious ideas that offered an alternative to the Sunni orthodoxy of Baghdad. The stage was being set for a new and far more radical rebellion, one that would not just seize Bahrain, but would turn it into the capital of a revolutionary republic that would terrorize the Abbasid world.

CHAPTER FIVE: The Qarmatian Republic: A Challenge to Abbasid Authority

As the 9th century drew to a close, the authority of the Abbasid Caliphate in Baghdad was fraying. From the opulent palaces of the capital, the Caliph's power seemed immense, but in the provinces, it was a different story. Decades of rebellion, economic strain, and the rising power of military warlords had weakened the empire's foundations. In the sun-scorched lands of eastern Arabia, a region the Abbasids had always struggled to fully control, this weakness created a vacuum. It was here, amongst the pearl fishers of the islands, the date farmers of the oases, and the Bedouin tribes of the desert, that a new and terrifying revolutionary movement would take root. For nearly two centuries, Bahrain would become the heart of a radical utopian state that would not only defy the Caliph but would drench the Islamic world in blood.

The movement's origins lay not in Bahrain itself, but in the complex and fractious world of Shi'a Islam. Specifically, it emerged from the Isma'ili branch, which held that the line of imams, the divinely guided successors to the Prophet Muhammad, had continued through his descendant Isma'il ibn Ja'far. The Isma'ilis were a messianic and esoteric sect, believing that the Quran had both an outer, literal meaning and an inner, hidden truth, which could only be revealed by the Imam. In the late 9th century, a missionary named Hamdan Qarmat began preaching a revolutionary version of this doctrine in southern Iraq. His followers, who became known as Qarmatians, believed the era of conventional Islamic law was ending and that the appearance of a prophesied savior, the Mahdi, was imminent. Their message was radical: a new world order was coming, one that would sweep away the corrupt Abbasid regime and establish a society of true equality and justice.

This potent ideology found its most effective champion in a man named Abu Sa'id al-Jannabi. A Persian from the coast of Fars, Abu Sa'id was trained as a missionary in Iraq before being dispatched to the wider Bahrain region around the year 899. He was a brilliant organizer and a charismatic leader, and he found fertile ground for his revolutionary message. Exploiting deep-seated grievances against the tax collectors and absentee landlords of the Abbasid state, he won over the powerful local tribes and the settled populations of the oases. He promised a utopian society where property would be held in common and the state would provide for all its citizens. It was an intoxicating vision for the poor and marginalized.

Abu Sa'id's movement quickly transitioned from underground mission to open rebellion. With an army of fiercely loyal Bedouin warriors, he began conquering the towns and oases of the region. In 900, he scored a major victory against an Abbasid army sent from Baghdad to crush his fledgling movement. A few years later, he captured the regional capital, Hajar, and established his new headquarters in the sprawling oasis of Al-Ahsa, which he made the capital of his new state. Bahrain, with its islands and ports, fell under his control, becoming a vital component of what is often called the Qarmatian Republic. It was not a republic in the modern sense, but it was a radical departure from the absolute monarchy of the Caliphate. The state was governed by a council of six, with Abu Sa'id serving as a chief among equals.

The society Abu Sa'id and his successors created was one of the most unusual experiments in the region's history. It was a highly organized, authoritarian, and collectivist state. All revenues from land, trade, and the pearl industry went into a central treasury. Private property was largely abolished. The state provided for its citizens, granting loans to the poor and those in debt without charging interest. According to one 11th-century visitor, the agricultural estates were worked by some thirty thousand enslaved people of East African origin, and the citizens of the capital were exempt from taxes. It was a society built on a rigid hierarchy and communal ownership, sustained by a slave-based economy and the spoils of war.

This utopian project was financed by relentless and extraordinarily brutal military campaigns. The Qarmatians saw the Abbasid Caliphate and the Sunni orthodoxy it represented as fundamentally illegitimate. From their base in eastern Arabia, they launched a series of devastating raids that terrorized the Middle East for decades. They considered the pilgrimage to Mecca a superstition and the routes across Arabia became their primary targets. In 906, they ambushed a pilgrim caravan returning from Mecca, slaughtering an estimated 20,000 people.

Abu Sa'id was assassinated in 913, but the leadership of the state passed to his sons. The most formidable of them was his youngest, Abu Tahir al-Jannabi, who took full command in 923. Barely a teenager, Abu Tahir was a military genius, possessed of both tactical brilliance and utter ruthlessness. He immediately escalated the war against the Abbasids, launching daring raids deep into Iraq. He sacked the great port city of Basra, ravaged the town of Kufa, and in 928, even threatened the imperial capital of Baghdad itself, before turning back to plunder the Iraqi countryside. The Abbasid armies seemed powerless to stop him.

Abu Tahir's reign culminated in the single most shocking act of the Qarmatian era. In January 930, during the height of the annual Hajj pilgrimage, he led his army to the holy city of Mecca. Gaining entry under the pretense of peace, he unleashed his soldiers on the unsuspecting pilgrims. For days, the city was a scene of carnage. The Qarmatians rode their horses into the Grand Mosque, cutting down worshippers as they prayed. They desecrated the sacred Zamzam Well, choking it with the corpses of the slain. According to some reports, as many as 30,000 pilgrims were massacred, their bodies left to rot in the streets.

The sacrilege did not end there. In a final, climactic act of defiance, Abu Tahir ordered his men to pry the sacred Black Stone from the corner of the Kaaba. This ancient relic, revered by Muslims as a link to the time of Abraham and Adam, was hoisted away. The Qarmatians carried it back across the desert to their capital in Al-Ahsa, along with immense treasures looted from the holy city. The attack on Mecca was a profound shock to the entire

Islamic world. For the Qarmatians, it was a symbolic act of immense power. By stealing the Black Stone, they believed they were signaling the end of the era of Islam and inaugurating a new age, with their state at its center. They intended to redirect the pilgrimage from Mecca to their own capital, though this effort ultimately failed as pilgrims continued to venerate the spot where the stone had been.

The Black Stone remained in Qarmatian hands for over two decades. The Abbasids, and even the Isma'ili Fatimid Caliphs in North Africa—who were theological rivals of the Qarmatians—repeatedly tried to persuade Abu Tahir to return it, but he refused. His actions were driven by a messianic fervor that soon took an even stranger turn. In 931, Abu Tahir declared a young Persian prisoner to be the long-awaited Mahdi. However, this new messiah proved to be a disaster, ordering the execution of notables and reportedly engaging in bizarre and anti-Islamic practices, including the worship of fire. The episode was a catastrophic miscalculation. The "Mahdi" was so destructive that Abu Tahir was forced to have him killed, a move that created a severe ideological crisis within the Qarmatian movement from which it never fully recovered.

Abu Tahir died in 944, and was succeeded by his brothers. The movement, shaken by the false Mahdi affair and facing increasing external pressure, began to lose its revolutionary momentum. Its leaders became more pragmatic. In 951, faced with a large ransom payment from the Abbasids, the Qarmatians finally returned the Black Stone. According to the historian al-Juwayni, it was unceremoniously dumped in the mosque at Kufa, wrapped in a sack with a note that read, "By command we took it, and by command we have brought it back." The abduction and rough handling had caused the stone to break into seven pieces.

The return of the stone marked the beginning of the end for the Qarmatian state. Their military power began to wane. They were defeated in a major battle by an Abbasid army in 976, which severely curtailed their ability to raid and extract tribute from their neighbors. The republic, deprived of its main source of income, began to shrink. Internal revolts started to break its authority apart.

Around 1058, a rebellion broke out on the Bahrain islands, led by local Shi'a chieftains from the Abd al-Qays tribe who successfully re-established orthodox rule.

The final blow came from the mainland. A powerful local chief named Abdullah bin Ali Al-Uyuni, with military backing from the rising Seljuk Empire, laid siege to the Qarmatian capital at Al-Ahsa. After a grueling seven-year siege, the city fell in 1076. The Qarmatian state, which had terrorized the Caliphate and challenged the very foundations of Islamic orthodoxy for more than a century and a half, was finally extinguished. Its radical experiment in communal living and military expansion was over, and a new era of local dynastic rule was about to begin.

CHAPTER SIX: The Age of Local Dynasties: Uyunids, Usfurids, and Jarwanids

The dramatic collapse of the Qarmatian state in 1076 inaugurated a new and complex chapter in the history of Bahrain. For nearly four centuries, the region would be governed not by distant caliphs or revolutionary ideologues, but by a succession of homegrown Arab dynasties. Power, once wielded by a messianic council in Al-Ahsa, now fell into the hands of local sheikhs and tribal leaders who, to varying degrees, controlled the fertile oases of the mainland and the pearl-rich islands. This era, stretching from the late 11th century to the cusp of the 16th, was a period of intense localism, shifting allegiances, and remarkable cultural developments, particularly in the religious identity of the populace. It was an age defined by three main ruling houses: the Uyunids, the Usfurids, and the Jarwanids, each leaving a distinct imprint on the region's character.

The man who single-handedly brought down the Qarmatian Republic was Abdullah bin Ali Al-Uyuni, a powerful sheikh from the local Abd al-Qays tribe. The Qarmatians, long stripped of their revolutionary fire, had become a decaying regional power, their income from raiding expeditions having dried up after a decisive defeat by the Abbasids in 976. Their authority was already crumbling from within; a revolt on the Bahrain islands around 1058 had already re-established orthodox rule there. Sensing the terminal decline of the old regime, Abdullah Al-Uyuni sought external backing for his own ambitions. He petitioned both the Abbasid Caliph in Baghdad and, more importantly, his powerful protector, the Seljuk Sultan Malik-Shah I. The Seljuks, a Turkic dynasty that now controlled much of Persia and Iraq, were eager to eradicate the last vestiges of the notorious Isma'ili state and extend their own influence into Arabia.

With the crucial support of Seljuk and other Abbasid-aligned forces, Abdullah launched his campaign. After a grueling seven-year siege, he captured the Qarmatian capital at Al-Ahsa in 1076, extinguishing the movement that had once made caliphs tremble. For his victory, Abdullah was recognized as the ruler of a new state, the Uyunid Emirate, which at its height encompassed the Bahrain islands, Qatif, and the Al-Ahsa oasis. Though he had relied on foreign steel to win his throne, he established a thoroughly local dynasty that would rule for more than a century and a half.

The Uyunid period was one of reconstruction and reconnection with the wider Islamic world. After the militant heresy of the Qarmatians, the Uyunids brought the region back into the fold of mainstream Islam. While their precise sectarian affiliation is debated by scholars—some sources suggest they were Sunni, others Twelver Shia—their rule coincided with a period when Twelver Shi'ism may have become more widespread among the populace of Eastern Arabia. Under Uyunid patronage, mosques were built, including the famous Al-Khamis Mosque, which was reconstructed during their era. One of the most celebrated poets in Bahrain's history, Ali bin al-Mugrab Al-Uyuni, was a member of the ruling family, and his work provides a rich, if partisan, account of the dynasty's triumphs and tribulations.

Despite their initial success, the Uyunid state was plagued by the persistent affliction of dynastic rule: internal family feuds. The founder's son, Al-Fadl, expanded the state's influence and at times moved the capital from the mainland to the islands, a testament to Bahrain's enduring importance. However, after the assassination of a later ruler in the 12th century, the emirate split into two competing branches, one based in Qatif and the other in Al-Ahsa. This division fatally weakened the dynasty, making it vulnerable to both internal rivals and external predators. The family squabbles were relentless, with power frequently changing hands through assassination and intrigue. This instability eventually opened the door for their overthrow. The final blow came in 1235, when the Persian ruler of Fars briefly occupied the archipelago, shattering what remained of Uyunid authority. By 1253, the last Uyunid ruler was deposed, and a new power emerged from the Bedouin tribes of the interior.

This new dynasty was the Usfurids, who hailed from the Banu Uqayl, a branch of the great Banu Amir tribal confederation. Unlike the Uyunids, who came from the long-settled Abd al-Qays tribe, the Usfurids were of a more nomadic background. Their founder, Usfur ibn Rashid, took advantage of the Uyunid collapse to establish his own authority, gaining control over the Al-Ahsa oasis and soon after, the rest of the former Uyunid domains, including the Bahrain islands.

The nature of Usfurid rule was likely different from that of their predecessors. It appears to have been less a centralized state and more of a tribal confederation, with power resting on the military strength of the Banu Uqayl and their allies. They navigated a complex geopolitical landscape, caught between the declining power of the Abbasids in Baghdad and the rising influence of Persian-based powers, such as the Ilkhanate (the Mongol successor state in Persia) and the maritime Kingdom of Hormuz. For a time, the Usfurids maintained their independence, with records showing them raiding as far as Basra in 1354 and clashing with Mongol forces.

However, their grip on the profitable Bahrain islands was often tenuous. The archipelago, with its lucrative pearl fisheries, was a glittering prize for any regional power. By the early 14th century, the merchants and princes of the Kingdom of Hormuz, which controlled the strategic strait at the mouth of the Gulf, began to exert their influence. Around 1320, Hormuz took control of Bahrain and Qatif, forcing the Usfurids to retreat to their heartland in Al-Ahsa. For much of the 14th century, the islands existed in a state of flux, with various powers, including the rulers of Hormuz and the Usfurids on the mainland, vying for the tribute generated by the pearl trade. This period of instability and fragmented authority set the stage for the rise of the region's third major local dynasty.

Sometime in the 14th century, the Usfurids were supplanted by the Jarwanids, a dynasty whose origins are somewhat obscure. Based in Qatif, the Jarwanids are believed to have belonged to the Bani Malik clan. Under their rule, the political and, crucially, the religious character of the region underwent a significant transformation. Contemporary sources describe the Jarwanids in no uncertain terms as "extreme Rawafidh," a polemical term for Shia Muslims who rejected the legitimacy of the first three caliphs.

While the Qarmatians had been Isma'ili Shia, the Jarwanids promoted the Twelver branch of Shi'ism, which would become the dominant faith of the native Bahraini population. Unlike the Qarmatians, who had suppressed conventional Islamic practices, the Jarwanids restored them, but with a distinctly Shia character. Mosques held regular prayers, and the call to prayer was made according to the Shia formula. Twelver scholars were appointed to important judicial and administrative posts. Historian Juan Cole has noted that "perhaps nowhere else in the Islamic world of the fourteenth century did Imami [Twelver] Shi'is have the kind of freedom and institutional position they possessed in Jarwanid Bahrain and East Arabia." The Jarwanid era was thus a pivotal moment in consolidating the region's Shia identity.

Like the Usfurids before them, the Jarwanids had to contend with the powerful Kingdom of Hormuz. For much of their reign, they ruled as vassals of the Hormuzi kings, paying tribute in exchange for a degree of local autonomy. This arrangement allowed them to control the internal affairs of Bahrain and the mainland oases while the Hormuzis, a great trading power, profited from the region's pearling wealth and maritime commerce.

The age of these local dynasties came to an end in the 15th century with the arrival of yet another tribal power from the Arabian interior, the Jabrids. Like the Usfurids, the Jabrids were descendants of the Banu Uqayl and were of Najdi origin. In the early 15th century, the first Jabrid ruler overthrew the last Jarwanid ruler in Qatif. Unlike the Shia Jarwanids, the Jabrids were staunch Sunni Muslims of the Maliki school. Under their most famous ruler, Ajwad ibn Zamil, who died around 1507, the

Jabrids built the most powerful state in the region's recent history. At their peak, they controlled the entire Arabian coast of the Gulf, from Kuwait to Qatar, including the Bahrain islands, and led regular military expeditions into central Arabia and Oman. One contemporary scholar described Ajwad ibn Zamil as "the king of al-Ahsa and Qatif and the leader of the people of Najd."

The Jabrids restored Sunni dominance to the region, but their timing was unfortunate. Just as their power reached its zenith, a new and unfamiliar flag appeared over the horizon. After the death of Ajwad ibn Zamil, his kingdom was divided among his descendants, weakening it at a critical moment. His grandson, Muqrin ibn Zamil, inherited rule over Al-Ahsa, Qatif, and Bahrain. It was Muqrin who would face the first wave of European colonial expansion into the Gulf. In 1521, a fleet of Portuguese warships, allied with their vassals from Hormuz, sailed for Bahrain. The age of local dynastic rule was about to be brought to a violent and abrupt end by the cannon fire of a new global power.

CHAPTER SEVEN: The Portuguese Era: A Century of European Control

For centuries, Bahrain's fate had been tied to the ambitions of its neighbors. Control shifted between dynasties based in Mesopotamia, Persia, and the Arabian mainland. Foreign influence was a constant, but it was a familiar kind of foreign. Then, at the dawn of the 16th century, a new and utterly alien power appeared on the horizon. From over the ocean came tall ships, their profiles unlike any seen in the Gulf, bristling with cannons that fired with devastating effect. These were the ships of the Kingdom of Portugal, a small European nation with a seemingly limitless appetite for spice, pearls, and empire. Their arrival in the Indian Ocean was less a voyage of discovery and more a maritime blitzkrieg, and it would not be long before their armored soldiers cast their acquisitive gaze upon the pearl-rich waters of Bahrain.

The Portuguese eruption into the East was the project of visionaries and warlords, most famously Afonso de Albuquerque, the second governor of the *Estado da Índia*, or State of India. His grand strategy was simple and brutal: to seize control of the key maritime choke points and shatter the existing Muslim-controlled trade networks that had supplied Europe with Eastern luxuries for centuries. With terrifying speed, his fleets captured Goa on the coast of India, Malacca in the straits of Southeast Asia, and in 1515, the crown jewel of the Gulf: the island kingdom of Hormuz. Hormuz, a bustling and cosmopolitan trading hub, became the linchpin of Portugal's Gulf strategy. From its formidable fortress, the Portuguese could dominate the sea lanes, tax the flow of commerce, and project power onto the surrounding coasts. And one of the most valuable dependencies of Hormuz was Bahrain.

The islands were then under the rule of Muqrin ibn Zamil, the last effective ruler of the Jabrid dynasty. Based on the mainland in Al-Ahsa, Muqrin presided over a domain that included the lucrative pearl fisheries of Bahrain and Qatif. He was a sovereign ruler, but the Portuguese, viewing the world through the lens of their vassalage over Hormuz, considered Bahrain to be a rebellious part of the Hormuzi kingdom. More pointedly, Muqrin refused to pay tribute to the Portuguese-Hormuzi alliance, a clear challenge to their new, self-proclaimed authority. For the Portuguese, this defiance, combined with the immense wealth generated by the pearl trade, made the conquest of Bahrain a strategic necessity. The King of Hormuz, likely under considerable Portuguese pressure, formally requested assistance in reclaiming his "lost" territory, providing the perfect pretext for an invasion.

In 1521, the expedition set sail. The commander was António Correia, the son of an explorer who had participated in the earlier bombardment of Calicut. Under his command was a combined force of Portuguese soldiers and ships from their Hormuzi vassal. They landed and were met by the forces of Muqrin ibn Zamil, who had crossed from the mainland to defend his island territory. The ensuing battle was a clash of military technologies. The Jabrid army, though courageous, was ultimately no match for the firepower of the Portuguese. Early in the fight, Muqrin was struck in the thigh by a musket ball, a severe wound that forced his withdrawal. Without their leader, the Jabrid forces collapsed. Bahrain was sacked, and its ships were burned.

Muqrin lingered for several days before succumbing to his wounds. What followed was a grim illustration of 16th-century warfare. His body was taken, and his head was severed and sent back to Hormuz as a trophy. The victorious commander, António Correia, was so proud of this achievement that he was granted the right to add the bleeding, decapitated head of Muqrin ibn Zamil to his family's coat of arms, a macabre symbol still featured by his descendants in Portugal. The Jabrid kingdom on the mainland crumbled soon after, leaving Bahrain firmly in the hands of the invaders. The brutal conquest marked a significant turning point: Bahrain became one of the first territories in the Middle East to fall under the direct colonial control of a European power.

The Portuguese established their rule, which would last for eighty years, but it was largely a form of indirect control. They relied on a series of governors, usually Sunni Persians loyal to their vassal in Hormuz, to manage the day-to-day affairs of the islands. This created a double layer of foreign domination that was deeply unpopular with Bahrain's largely Shia Arab population, who suffered under the new administration. The primary Portuguese interest was not in governance but in profit. Their goal was to monopolize the fabulous wealth of the pearl fisheries, diverting the revenue into the coffers of Hormuz and, ultimately, Lisbon.

To secure their prize, the Portuguese set about fortifying their position. They took over the ancient tell at Qal'at al-Bahrain, a site that had been the capital of Dilmun millennia before, and began constructing a massive fort. This structure, which still dominates the northern coastline, was a classic European-style military fortification, a stone declaration of their power and permanence. It served as the base for the Portuguese garrison, a tangible symbol of their control over the island and its trade routes.

Portuguese-Hormuzi rule was often characterized by greed and cruelty, which predictably bred resentment and resistance. The eighty-year occupation was punctuated by a series of bloody rebellions. The first major uprising occurred in 1529, when demands for higher tribute payments became unbearable. The revolt was serious enough that the Portuguese Viceroy in Goa had to dispatch a force of 400 men to violently suppress it and restore order. The local population's hatred for their occupiers simmered, with one Hormuzi governor reportedly being crucified by rebels. This constant state of unrest demonstrated the tenuousness of Portuguese control, which was dependent on their naval power and the formidable walls of their fort.

The Portuguese were not the only major power in the region. To the north, the Ottoman Empire was also expanding. Having conquered Egypt and much of the Arabian Peninsula, their influence was creeping down the Gulf coast. The Ottomans saw the Portuguese as infidel intruders and commercial rivals, and for several decades, the two empires clashed in a series of naval engagements across the Indian Ocean. By the 1550s, the Ottomans had established a province in Al-Ahsa on the mainland, making them direct neighbors to Portuguese Bahrain.

In 1559, the local Ottoman governor, Mustafa Pasha, decided to take matters into his own hands. Assembling a force of around 1,200 soldiers and a fleet of galleys and transport ships, he launched an invasion of Bahrain, aiming to capture the fort and wrest control of the pearl trade from the Portuguese. The Ottoman troops landed in July and laid siege to the fortress at Manama. The fort's commander, a Hormuzi governor named Murad Shah, held out with his garrison of 400 mercenaries and sent an urgent message for help to the main Portuguese base at Hormuz.

The Portuguese relief force, commanded by Álvaro da Silveira, managed to outwit the Ottoman fleet. Approaching from an unexpected direction, they launched a surprise attack, capturing the Ottoman ships and trapping Mustafa Pasha's army on the island. The land campaign, however, proved more difficult. The Turks retreated into the island's palm groves, and a bloody stalemate ensued. The siege dragged on for months, with both sides suffering heavy casualties not only from fighting but also from a devastating outbreak of plague that swept through both camps. By November, the exhausted and disease-ridden Ottoman force offered terms. After paying a ransom and surrendering their arms, the few hundred survivors were allowed to withdraw. The failed siege marked the high-water mark of the Ottoman threat to Bahrain and effectively secured Portuguese hegemony in the Gulf for another four decades.

The power that would ultimately drive the Portuguese from Bahrain was not the Ottomans, but a resurgent Persia under the Safavid dynasty. Shah Abbas I, one of Persia's most formidable rulers, was determined to restore his empire's influence and expel the Portuguese from the Gulf. He began by consolidating his control over the Persian mainland, capturing the province of Lar in 1601, which gave him a strategic position on the coast.

The opportunity to seize Bahrain came a year later, in 1602, through a combination of local intrigue and Persian opportunism. The Hormuzi governor of Bahrain, Rukn al-Din Mas'ud, had alienated the local population, reportedly by executing some of the island's wealthiest merchants. This sparked a popular uprising.

Fearing retaliation from the Portuguese garrison in the fort, Rukn al-Din sought military aid from the Safavid general Allahverdi Khan, the governor of the nearby Persian province of Fars. Allahverdi Khan, acting on Shah Abbas's expansionist ambitions, saw the perfect chance to intervene.

He dispatched a force of musketeers who, likely with the support of the local population, helped the rebels expel the Portuguese garrison from the fort. Rukn al-Din may have believed he had secured his own independence, but his Persian allies had other ideas. Once the Portuguese were gone, Allahverdi Khan promptly had Rukn al-Din executed and claimed the islands for the Safavid Empire. A Portuguese attempt to retake the island with a fleet from Hormuz was repelled, and their eighty-year rule came to an abrupt end. The fall of Bahrain in 1602 was a major blow to the Portuguese *Estado da Índia* and a precursor to their loss of Hormuz to a combined Persian and English force twenty years later. The era of European control was over, for now, but the formidable stone fort they left behind would stand for centuries as the most enduring legacy of their violent and rapacious tenure.

CHAPTER EIGHT: Persian and Omani Contests for the Islands

The expulsion of the Portuguese in 1602 did not bring Bahrain lasting independence, but rather a change in overlords. The formidable stone fort at Qal'at al-Bahrain, once the symbol of European intrusion, now housed a Persian garrison. For the next century and a half, the islands' destiny would be inextricably linked to the fortunes of Persia, first under the powerful Safavid dynasty and later under its turbulent successors. This long era of Persian suzerainty was not, however, one of quiet submission. It was punctuated by foreign invasion, local rebellion, and economic ruin, as a new and ambitious maritime power, the Imamate of Oman, rose to challenge Persian dominance in the Gulf. For the people of Bahrain, it was a period of being caught between two mighty regional rivals, a struggle that would ultimately create the power vacuum from which a new local dynasty would emerge.

Under Shah Abbas I, the ruler who had driven out the Portuguese, Bahrain was absorbed into the Safavid Empire. For the predominantly Shia Arab population of the islands, this was a significant shift. Their new rulers were not Catholic Europeans or Sunni Hormuzis, but the head of the world's great Shia empire. This shared religious identity fostered a unique relationship. The Safavids sought to control Bahrain not just by military force, but through ideology, reinforcing the religious ties between the islands' clerics and the great centers of learning in Persia. Safavid rule was generally indirect, with authority delegated to local Arab sheikhs or Persian governors who were tasked with collecting tribute and maintaining order. This period was an intellectual golden age for Bahrain's theological elite, as its seminaries flourished, producing renowned scholars whose influence was felt across the Shia world. The economy, as always, revolved around the pearl trade, and the Safavids were content to profit from this commerce while leaving its day-to-day management in local hands.

This relatively stable arrangement depended entirely on the strength of the Safavid state. By the early 18th century, that strength was rapidly fading. The empire was beset by internal decay, and its frontiers were threatened by Afghan invaders who, in 1722, would succeed in sacking the capital, Isfahan. The chaos at the heart of the empire was felt acutely in its peripheral territories. Seeing the Persian grip on the Gulf weaken, another power sensed an opportunity. From their capital in Muscat, the Yaruba dynasty of Oman had built a formidable maritime empire, having already expelled the Portuguese from their own shores and expanded their influence down the coast of East Africa. Now, they looked north.

In 1717, the Imam of Oman, Sultan bin Saif II, launched a naval invasion of Bahrain. For the Bahrainis, the attack was a terrifying ordeal. A contemporary account from the Bahraini theologian Sheikh Yusuf Al Bahrani describes a desperate and bloody struggle. The Omanis, whom he refers to as Kharijites, failed in their first two attempts to take the island. On their third try, they blockaded the archipelago, starving its inhabitants into submission. The final assault was a "horrific battle and a terrible catastrophe," marked by widespread "killing, plunder, pillage, and bloodshed." The invasion brought an end to 115 years of Safavid hegemony. Many of the island's notables, including Sheikh Al Bahrani's father, fled the chaos. The Omanis established direct rule, appointing their own governors and imposing heavy taxes, which soon drove away many of the pearl merchants and divers who were the lifeblood of the economy.

The Omani occupation was a period of instability and destruction. An attempt by the Persians, with the help of Bedouin allies, to retake the islands failed miserably and resulted in much of the country being burned to the ground. The Omani conquest began what one historian has called a "century of madness," an era of constant warfare that laid waste to much of Bahrain. The population plummeted. The German geographer Carsten Niebuhr, visiting in 1763, observed that the 360 towns and villages that had once dotted the islands had been reduced to just 60 through conflict and economic collapse.

Persia, however, was not gone for good. The collapse of the Safavids had paved the way for the rise of one of the most brilliant and ruthless military commanders in Iranian history: Nadir Shah. A man of humble origins, Nadir rose to become the undisputed ruler of Persia, founding the Afsharid dynasty and launching a series of ambitious campaigns to restore and expand the empire. A core part of his strategy was to establish Persian naval supremacy in the Gulf, a goal for which the recapture of Bahrain was an essential first step. In 1736, he ordered his admiral, Latif Khan, to assemble an invasion fleet at the port of Bushehr. The Persians landed in March or April while Bahrain's ruler, Shaikh Jubayr, was away on the Hajj pilgrimage. The invasion was a success, dislodging the Omanis and bringing the islands back under Persian rule.

Nadir Shah's ambitions did not stop at Bahrain. He intended to make Persia the undisputed power of the Gulf. His newly built navy went on to attack Omani holdings, even conquering Muscat itself in 1743. For Bahrain, however, rule under the iron-fisted Nadir Shah was likely no gentler than it had been under the Omanis. His empire was built on constant warfare, which was funded by relentless taxation of his subjects. But his reign, like his life, was destined to be short and violent. In 1747, he was assassinated by his own officers, and Persia was once again plunged into a bloody civil war.

This new power vacuum in Persia created an opportunity for a different kind of ruler to emerge in the Gulf. Without a strong central authority, local and regional leaders began to assert their independence. This was particularly true of the Arab tribes living on the Persian coast, a group collectively known as the Huwala. Having migrated from Arabia centuries earlier, these Sunni Arab mariners, merchants, and pearl divers had become a significant political and economic force in the coastal ports. One of the most powerful of these groups was the Al Madhkur family, who ruled the strategic port city of Bushehr.

Following Nadir Shah's death, Persia was eventually reunified under the more moderate rule of Karim Khan Zand. Seeking to re-establish Persian influence in the Gulf without the expense of direct military campaigns, Karim Khan outsourced the governance of Bahrain. Around 1753, the islands were occupied by the Al Madhkur family of Bushehr, who ruled in the name of the Persian Shah. The sheikh of Bushehr, Nasr Al-Madhkur, became the effective governor of Bahrain, paying allegiance and tribute to the Zand dynasty in Shiraz. For the next three decades, Bahrain was a dependency of an Arab sheikhdom on the Persian coast, which was itself a vassal of the Persian king.

This arrangement, however, did little to bring stability. To observers like Carsten Niebuhr, Sheikh Nasr Al-Madhkur appeared to be the "sole Monarch of the isle of Bahrain," ruling his domain as a practically independent state. But his authority was constantly being tested. The mid-18th century was a time of shifting alliances and rising tribal powers. On the nearby coast of the Qatar peninsula, a confederation of Arab tribes known as the Bani Utbah had established a thriving new town at Zubarah. Their growing commercial success and military strength were beginning to attract the attention of the region's established powers.

The prosperity of Zubarah was a direct challenge to rulers like Sheikh Nasr, who saw it as a threat to their own commercial interests. Tensions simmered for years, finally boiling over in 1782. The spark was a minor dispute on the island of Sitra that escalated and resulted in the death of a member of the Al Khalifa family, one of the leading clans of the Bani Utbah. In response, Sheikh Nasr Al-Madhkur assembled a large invasion force, estimated at two to four thousand men, and laid siege to Zubarah, demanding the town's surrender. The siege failed. The Bani Utbah and their local allies mounted a fierce defense and repelled the attack.

The failed siege was a turning point. Humiliated and defeated, Sheikh Nasr retreated to his ships and returned to Bushehr. The following year, 1783, the Bani Utbah went on the offensive. Led by Sheikh Ahmed ibn Muhammad Al Khalifa, a fleet sailed from Zubarah to Bahrain. They defeated Al-Madhkur's forces, captured the great fort, and for the first time, brought the islands under the rule of the Al Khalifa. Attempts by the Persians to organize a counter-attack failed due to the death of their ruler, Karim Khan's successor, which plunged the country back into internal chaos. After nearly two centuries of being a pawn in the strategic contests of distant empires, Bahrain was now in the hands of a new power, one that had risen from the shores of Arabia itself.

CHAPTER NINE: The Rise of the Al Khalifa

The year 1783 was a watershed. For the first time in nearly three centuries, since the brief interregnum of the Jabrids, Bahrain was in the hands of an Arab power that was not a vassal to a foreign empire. The victory of the Bani Utbah tribal confederation, led by Sheikh Ahmed ibn Muhammad Al Khalifa, was more than a mere changing of the guard at the old Portuguese fort; it was the genesis of a new political entity, one born not in Shiraz or Muscat, but on the shores of the Gulf itself. The defeat of the Persian-backed forces of Bushehr marked the end of an era of being a pawn in the games of others and the beginning of a new one, in which the islands' destiny would be shaped by a dynasty that would tie its own fate to that of Bahrain. This was not a simple conquest, but the culmination of a decades-long migration that saw a clan of desert Arabs transform themselves into masters of a maritime state.

The story of the Al Khalifa begins not on the sea, but deep in the arid interior of Arabia, in the Najd. They belong to the Anizah, a large and powerful tribal confederation that has roamed the Arabian desert for centuries. In the 17th century, a severe drought prompted a wave of migrations out of the desiccated heartland towards the more fertile peripheries. Among these migrants were a group of clans who banded together for mutual protection and enterprise, a confederation that came to be known as the Bani Utbah. This alliance, whose name may mean "the ones who wandered," included the ancestors of three future ruling families: the Al Sabah, the Al Jalahma, and the Al Khalifa. Moving north and east, they were at times raiders and mercenaries, eventually making their way to the coast of the Persian Gulf.

Around the beginning of the 18th century, the Bani Utbah settled in the small port town of Kuwait. Here, they found their footing as merchants, mariners, and pearl fishers, honing the skills that would define their future. For several decades, the clans coexisted, with the Al Sabah eventually emerging as the pre-eminent family in Kuwait itself. Sometime in the 1760s, a significant portion of the Al Khalifa and Al Jalahma clans decided to seek their fortunes elsewhere. They migrated south down the coast to the Qatar peninsula, a sparsely populated region with promising pearl banks and a strategic location. There, near an abandoned settlement, they founded a new town: Zubarah.

Under the leadership of the Al Khalifa, Zubarah grew with astonishing speed. Strategically located, possessing a large natural harbor, and positioned near some of the Gulf's richest pearl beds, it was perfectly designed for commerce. It became a thriving free-trade port, attracting merchants and tribesmen from across the Gulf and the Indian Ocean. As a fortified coastal town, its impressive walls, towers, and forts protected the burgeoning settlement from rivals and raiders. Zubarah's prosperity was a direct challenge to the established order. Its success drew the envy of the Persian-backed rulers of Bahrain and Bushehr, who saw their own trade revenues being siphoned off by this upstart port. This commercial rivalry was the direct cause of the conflict that culminated in the 1782 siege of Zubarah and the Al Khalifa's counter-stroke against Bahrain the following year.

After his decisive victory, Sheikh Ahmed ibn Muhammad Al Khalifa became the first Al Khalifa ruler of Bahrain, earning the honorific title *al-Fatih*, or "the Conqueror." Yet, in a move that underscored the source of his power, he chose not to relocate to his newly won prize. He continued to reside in Zubarah, the commercial powerhouse he and his family had built, and governed Bahrain through appointed deputies. For Sheikh Ahmed, Bahrain was a vital and immensely valuable addition to his domain, but Zubarah remained its heart. The islands, with their vast date palm groves and legendary pearl banks, would now provide the revenue to secure the new dynasty's position.

This new order did not go unchallenged. The conquest had created a host of enemies who viewed the Al Khalifa as illegitimate usurpers. The Persians never relinquished their claim of sovereignty over the islands, a claim they would continue to press for the next two centuries. The Omanis, who had occupied Bahrain earlier in the century, also saw the Al Khalifa's rise as a threat to their own maritime ambitions and launched attacks in 1799 and 1800, attempting to retake the islands. A brief Omani occupation was successful, and the ruler of Muscat installed his young son as governor at Arad Fort, though the Al Khalifa, taking advantage of the Omani fleet's absence, managed to retake control a year later.

Within the Bani Utbah confederation itself, old rivalries festered. The Al Jalahma clan, led by the formidable Rahmah ibn Jabir al-Jalahimah, felt they had been cheated of their fair share of the spoils after the conquest. Holding a deep grudge against his Al Khalifa cousins, Rahmah ibn Jabir broke away and established his own coastal strongholds, first in Khor Hassan in Qatar and later in Dammam. For the next four decades, he would be a constant and menacing presence in the Gulf. Viewed by the British as a pirate but by others as a powerful sovereign chief, he waged a relentless naval war against Al Khalifa shipping, allying with anyone who shared his enmity towards the rulers of Bahrain.

However, the greatest threat was to come not from the sea, but from the desert interior. Sheikh Ahmed al-Fatih died in 1796, and his two eldest sons, Salman and Abdullah, succeeded him. They took the momentous decision to relocate the family from Zubarah to Bahrain, establishing their seats of power on the islands. Salman settled on the main island, while Abdullah was based on Muharraq. This move coincided with the dramatic expansion of a new, terrifying force from the Najd: the First Saudi State, driven by the puritanical and militant ideology of Wahhabism.

The Wahhabis, viewing the Shia population of the Gulf coast as heretics and the region's pearling wealth as a legitimate source of revenue, swept out of the desert in the late 18th century. In 1796, they captured the Al-Ahsa oasis and then occupied Zubarah, forcing the Al Khalifa to consolidate their power entirely on the islands. The once-thriving metropolis of Zubarah, cut off from its maritime rulers and now under the austere hand of the Wahhabis, went into a terminal decline. It was attacked and largely destroyed in 1811, its inhabitants scattered, and its walls left to be slowly covered by the desert sands.

For the Al Khalifa in Bahrain, the Wahhabi threat was existential. For several years, they were forced to pay tribute to the Saudi Emir to stave off an invasion. But by 1802, the pressure became unbearable. A Wahhabi army invaded the islands, and for a brief but traumatic period, Bahrain fell under the direct suzerainty of the Saudi state. The Al Khalifa were temporarily expelled, becoming rulers in exile. This crisis revealed the precariousness of their position and the complex web of regional rivalries. In a desperate bid to oust the Wahhabis, the Al Khalifa sought help from the Sultan of Muscat. The Omanis obliged, driving out the Saudi garrison in 1811, but then promptly tried to claim the islands for themselves, forcing the Al Khalifa to fight to regain their own patrimony.

It was during this chaotic period that the Al Khalifa, under the joint leadership of Sheikh Salman bin Ahmed and Sheikh Abdullah bin Ahmed, finally secured their independent rule. With the Wahhabi state now under attack in their heartland from a major Egyptian-Ottoman expedition, their power in the Gulf evaporated, allowing the Al Khalifa to re-establish their authority in Bahrain without fear of imminent invasion from the desert. The destruction of Zubarah and the trauma of the Wahhabi occupation cemented a new reality: Bahrain was no longer a dependency of a mainland power base; it *was* the power base. The family's identity and future were now wholly invested in the islands.

The system of joint rule between the brothers Salman and Abdullah, which had been forged in the crucible of war and exile, became the political template for the next generation. While it ensured a degree of unity against external threats, it also contained the seeds of future conflict. The two brothers had different temperaments; Salman was seen as more pragmatic and inclined towards commerce, while Abdullah was a more traditional and ambitious warrior-sheikh, keen to project power on the mainland and confront his rivals. Their descendants would form two competing branches of the family—the Al-Salman and the Al-

Abdullah—whose rivalry would dominate Bahrain's internal politics for much of the 19th century.

The decades following the Wahhabi withdrawal were a time of constant vigilance. The Omani navy remained a powerful force in the lower Gulf. Persia's claims, though unenforceable, were a persistent diplomatic nuisance. And the ever-present threat of Rahmah ibn Jabir's fleet required the Al Khalifa to maintain their own naval strength. Rahmah's long and bloody career finally came to an end in 1826 in a dramatic sea battle. Trapped and facing certain defeat at the hands of a fleet led by Sheikh Ahmed bin Salman Al Khalifa, the old warrior retreated to his ship's powder magazine and, in a final act of defiance, blew it up, killing himself, his young son, and all the Al Khalifa men who had boarded his vessel.

This volatile environment of dynastic feuds, regional power struggles, and endemic maritime warfare was drawing the attention of a new and far more powerful player. On the seas of the Gulf, the ships of the British East India Company were becoming an ever-more-common sight. Their chief concern was not the conquest of territory, but the security of their trade routes to India, which were threatened by the constant state of war and so-called piracy. The internal conflicts of the Al Khalifa and their external struggles with their neighbours were increasingly seen as a disruptive influence. In 1820, seeking to impose a general peace on the region, British representatives signed a treaty with a number of Gulf sheikhs, including the Al Khalifa. This agreement, the first of many, was a pivotal moment. By signing it, Britain formally recognized the Al Khalifa as the legitimate rulers of Bahrain, a move that provided them with a powerful new shield against their regional rivals. It also marked the beginning of a long and complex relationship that would safeguard the dynasty's rule but would also, step by step, draw Bahrain into the orbit of the British Empire.

CHAPTER TEN: Pax Britannica: Treaties, Maritime Security, and British Influence

The Al Khalifa's hard-won victory in 1783 had secured the islands, but it had not secured a lasting peace. The dawn of the 19th century found Bahrain in a state of constant peril, its rulers navigating a sea of threats from vengeful Omanis, expansionist Wahhabis, and the ever-present, though currently dormant, claims of Persia. The dynasty's survival depended on its ability to play one rival against another, a dangerous game of shifting allegiances that offered little long-term security. Into this volatile environment sailed a new power, one whose interests were not in conquest but in control, not in territory but in trade. For the British Empire, the Persian Gulf was not a prize to be won but a vital artery to be secured. The sea route to India, the jewel in its imperial crown, had to be protected at all costs from the endemic piracy and tribal warfare that defined the region. This single strategic imperative would lead to a relationship that would dominate Bahrain's history for the next 150 years, creating a new order in the Gulf known as the *Pax Britannica*, or British Peace.

The first formal contact was driven by Britain's desire to eradicate what it saw as piracy. In the early 19th century, the waters of the lower Gulf were the domain of the Qawasim, a formidable maritime federation based in Ras Al Khaimah. While the Qawasim saw themselves as a sovereign naval power engaged in legitimate warfare, the British East India Company, whose ships were frequently attacked, saw only pirates. After a major naval expedition in 1819 destroyed the Qawasim fleet and sacked Ras Al Khaimah, Britain imposed a new order. In the smoldering ruins of the port, British officials compelled the defeated sheikhs to sign a document called the General Maritime Treaty of 1820. Its purpose was "the cessation of plunder and piracy by land and sea... for ever."

The rulers of Bahrain, having repeatedly asked for British support against their many rivals, willingly acceded to the treaty in

February 1820. For the Al Khalifa, the treaty was a strategic masterstroke. It was primarily an anti-piracy and anti-slavery agreement, but in signing it, Great Britain formally recognized them as the legitimate rulers of Bahrain. This was an invaluable endorsement, a powerful diplomatic shield against the Omani, Persian, and Ottoman claims that had haunted the dynasty since its inception. In return for pledging to abstain from "war, piracy, and slavery at sea," the Al Khalifa gained a powerful, if initially reluctant, patron. Britain, for its part, gained another partner in its quest to pacify the Gulf and secure its trade routes. This was not a colonial relationship, not yet, but the first critical thread in a web of obligations that would grow progressively tighter over the decades.

The treaty did not magically end all conflict. The Gulf remained a dangerous place, and Bahrain's rulers continued to face internal and external threats. The rivalry between the descendants of Sheikh Salman and Sheikh Abdullah frequently paralyzed the government and invited outside interference. The Wahhabis on the mainland remained a potent force, and Persia never missed an opportunity to reassert its ancient claim to sovereignty. Throughout this period, the Al Khalifa repeatedly sought a more formal protection agreement from the British, but London remained hesitant, preferring to keep the islands as an independent but friendly buffer state. The Royal Navy's Persian Gulf Squadron, based on Qishm Island, became the enforcer of the treaty, its gunboats a common sight in the waters off Manama, but its intervention was meant to police the seas, not the internal politics of the islands.

This policy of cautious distance began to change in the middle of the century. The ruler at the time, Sheikh Muhammad bin Khalifa, was a proud and ambitious leader who chafed under British restrictions. He sought to project his power onto the mainland, particularly against the Wahhabis in Dammam and their allies in Qatar. To the British Political Resident in Bushehr, the chief British official in the Gulf, these independent military actions were a violation of the maritime peace. Sheikh Muhammad further alarmed the British by opening diplomatic channels with the

Ottoman and Persian empires, seeking their protection as a counterweight to British influence. This was precisely the kind of great-power rivalry the British wanted to prevent in the Gulf. The final straw came in 1861 when Sheikh Muhammad blockaded the Arabian coast, an act of war that Britain could not ignore.

The British response was swift and decisive. They forced Sheikh Muhammad to sign a new, more restrictive treaty, the Perpetual Truce of Peace and Friendship of 1861. This agreement went far beyond the 1820 treaty. In it, the ruler of Bahrain recognized the "perpetual ban on maritime warfare" and in return, Britain offered protection from "all aggression by sea." Crucially, the treaty explicitly forbade the ruler from ceding any part of his territory to another power and from entering into any relationship with a foreign government without British consent. This treaty marked a pivotal moment. Bahrain was now formally under British protection, its foreign policy effectively handed over to the British Crown in exchange for security. The islands had become a protectorate in all but name.

The new treaty was immediately put to the test, not by a foreign power, but by the ruler himself. In 1867, Sheikh Muhammad launched an attack on Qatar, which the British considered a clear violation of the truce. The Royal Navy intervened, bombarding his forces. Sheikh Muhammad fled, and the British, now the ultimate arbiters of power, oversaw the installation of his brother, Ali bin Khalifa, as the new ruler. The game of thrones did not end there. A year later, Sheikh Muhammad returned with supporters and killed Sheikh Ali in battle. This time, the British had lost all patience with the dynastic feuding. In 1869, the Political Resident, Colonel Lewis Pelly, sailed to Bahrain with a naval force. He arrested Sheikh Muhammad's partisans, exiled the rival claimants to India, and, after consulting with the senior members of the Al Khalifa, appointed a 21-year-old named Isa bin Ali Al Khalifa as the new ruler.

The accession of Sheikh Isa bin Ali marked the beginning of a new era of stability, albeit one underwritten by British power. His reign, which would last an extraordinary 63 years, coincided with the high watermark of the British Empire. With a British-approved ruler on the throne, external threats evaporated. The Royal Navy shielded Bahrain from any possibility of Omani or Persian invasion, and British diplomacy neutralized Ottoman ambitions. The *Pax Britannica* provided an unprecedented level of security, allowing the pearl industry to flourish and making Manama the pre-eminent commercial center of the Gulf.

This security, however, came at the cost of sovereignty. Step by step, Britain deepened its involvement in Bahrain's affairs. The internal family rivalries that had once been settled by open warfare were now mediated by the British Political Resident in Bushehr. Concerned by the growing influence of other European powers—particularly France, Germany, and Russia—in the region, Britain moved to formalize its exclusive position. In 1880, Sheikh Isa was compelled to sign a new agreement, pledging not to enter into negotiations or make treaties with any other foreign government without British consent. This was followed by the even more explicit Exclusive Agreement of 1892, which added a clause forbidding the ruler from ceding, selling, or mortgaging any part of his territory to any power other than the British Government. With these treaties, Bahrain's status as a British protectorate was sealed.

The tangible symbol of this growing influence was the establishment of a permanent British Political Agency in Bahrain in 1900. Previously, British interests had been managed from the residency across the Gulf in Bushehr. Now, a British official, the Political Agent, resided in Manama itself. He acted as the intermediary between the ruler and the British government, but his role quickly expanded. He became a sort of permanent, and powerful, advisor to Sheikh Isa. A two-storey agency building, with deep verandas and a courthouse, was constructed on the Manama shoreline, a physical manifestation of British authority.

The Political Agent's power was demonstrated most clearly through the exercise of legal jurisdiction. Following an incident in 1904 where a relative of the ruler attacked some German and Persian merchants, the British used the affair to pressure Sheikh Isa into formally placing all legal cases involving foreigners into

British hands. Through a series of Orders in Council issued in London, a parallel legal system was created, with British courts in Bahrain holding jurisdiction not only over British subjects but over a vast and vaguely defined category of "foreigners." This system was designed to protect British commercial interests, but it also fundamentally undermined the ruler's authority within his own country, creating a state within a state.

By the early 20th century, the relationship that had begun as a pragmatic alliance for maritime security had transformed into a full-blown colonial arrangement. The Al Khalifa dynasty was secure on the throne, protected from all external enemies and from the internal rivals who had plagued it for decades. But the ruler was no longer an independent sovereign. His foreign policy was dictated by London, his authority over foreigners was non-existent, and the ever-present advice of the British Political Agent was impossible to ignore. The peace that Britain had imposed upon the Gulf had preserved Bahrain's existence as a distinct political entity and secured the Al Khalifa's rule, but in the process, it had entangled the islands completely within the strategic and political orbit of the British Empire.

CHAPTER ELEVEN: The Pearl Industry: Boom, Bust, and Social Change

For millennia, the history of Bahrain was written in the iridescent shimmer of a single gem. Long before the first oil rig broke the horizon, the islands' economy, society, and very identity were shaped by the perilous pursuit of pearls. Archaeological evidence suggests pearling was practiced here as early as 2000 BC, during the age of Dilmun. Pliny the Elder wrote of Tylos being "famous for the vast number of its pearls," and for centuries thereafter, Bahrain's pearls were prized for their exceptional lustre and purity, qualities local lore attributed to the unique freshwater springs that bubble up beneath the salty seabed. The industry was not just a source of income; it was the organizing principle of life itself. The annual pearling season, the *ghaus*, dictated the rhythms of the year, and the wealth it generated—or failed to generate—determined the fate of nearly every family on the islands. By the 19th and early 20th centuries, this ancient trade had reached its zenith, transforming Bahrain into the glittering center of a global luxury market before a sudden and catastrophic collapse remade the nation forever.

The entire social calendar revolved around the pearling season. The main event was the *ghaus al-kabir*, the "great dive," a grueling four-and-a-half-month season that ran from June through early October, during the hottest and most humid months of the year. In the weeks prior, the towns of Manama and Muharraq, then the pearling capital of the Gulf, would be abuzz with activity. Boat owners, or *nakhudas*, would secure financing from wealthy merchants, known as *tawashin*, to outfit their dhows and provision them for the long journey. Divers and crew would take advances on their future earnings to support the families they were leaving behind. The day of departure, known as *al-dasha*, was a deeply emotional community event, with families gathering at the shore to bid farewell to the thousands of men setting sail for the oyster beds, or *hayrat*, knowing that not all would return.

Life aboard the pearling dhows was a study in hardship. A typical crew consisted of a rigid hierarchy. At the top was the *nakhuda*, the captain, who was the absolute master of the vessel and its men. Beneath him were the two most vital roles: the divers, the *ghais*, and their haulers, the *saib*. The rest of the crew was made up of apprentices, or *walad*, young boys who performed odd jobs and learned the trade, and often a singer, the *nahham*, who sang traditional songs to motivate the men and break the soul-crushing monotony of the work.

The diver's work was exceptionally dangerous and physically punishing. With only the most rudimentary equipment, they would descend to depths of up to 20 meters. Their tools were simple: a tortoiseshell or bone nose clip (*futam*), leather finger protectors (*khabt*) to shield against sharp coral, a weighted rope (*hajar*) to speed their descent, and a woven basket (*diyyin*) slung around their neck to hold the oysters. The diver would be lowered by the *saib*, his tender and partner on the rope. He would hold his breath for up to two minutes, frantically gathering as many oysters as he could before tugging on the rope to be hauled back to the surface, gasping for air before preparing for the next plunge. They made dozens of such dives from sunrise to sunset, their bodies exposed to sharks, jellyfish, the constant risk of drowning, and the crippling effects of the bends.

The economic structure that underpinned this immense labor was as unforgiving as the sea itself. It was a complex system of credit and debt that kept the vast majority of divers and crew in a state of perpetual bondage. The system was controlled by the *tawashin*, the wealthy pearl merchants who financed the entire industry. These merchants, whose grand coral-stone houses still grace the narrow alleyways of Muharraq, were the apex of the pearling society. They advanced money to the *nakhudas*, who in turn advanced money and supplies to their crew. These pre-season loans, or *salaf*, were essential for the divers' families to survive while they were at sea, but they came at a heavy price.

The loans were recorded in ledgers, but with exorbitant interest rates and a valuation system that was entirely controlled by the captain and merchant. At the end of the season, the value of the pearl catch was calculated. After the financier and the captain took their large shares, the diver's portion was tallied against his debt. It was seldom, if ever, enough to clear the loan. The remaining debt was carried over to the next season, growing year after year, locking the diver into a cycle of servitude from which there was virtually no escape. This debt was hereditary; a son would inherit his father's obligations along with his profession, ensuring a permanent labor pool for the pearling magnates. It was a system that generated fabulous wealth for a few, built upon the bonded labor of thousands.

For a time, the wealth was staggering. The late 19th and early 20th centuries were the golden age of Bahraini pearling. The security imposed by the *Pax Britannica* pacified the Gulf's waters, allowing the industry to flourish on an unprecedented scale. At its peak, the industry employed a vast portion of the male population, with thousands of boats and an estimated 30,000 men working the pearl banks each season. This boom coincided with the Gilded Age in America and the Belle Époque in Europe, eras of extravagant wealth and a voracious appetite for luxury goods. Natural pearls were more precious than diamonds, and Bahrain was the undisputed source of the world's finest.

By 1905, an estimated 97% of the Gulf's entire pearl turnover was traded through Bahrain. The value of its pearl exports sextupled between 1900 and 1912. The suqs of Manama and Muharraq became magnets for international jewelers. Agents for European firms set up offices in the city. The most famous among them was Jacques Cartier, who visited Bahrain in 1912 to establish direct links with the local merchants, seeking to bypass the intermediaries in Bombay and secure the best gems for the famous French jewelry house. His visit cemented Bahrain's reputation as the global capital of the pearl trade. Black and white photographs from his trip capture a lost world: Cartier, dressed in a suit, sitting on a dhow surrounded by powerful Bahraini merchants, the very men who controlled the flow of this immense wealth.

Then, in the space of a few short years, this entire world collapsed. The fall was swift, brutal, and came from two directions at once. The first and most fatal blow came from Japan. For years, a persistent entrepreneur named Kokichi Mikimoto had been experimenting with a revolutionary idea: forcing an oyster to create a pearl by artificially inserting a nucleus. After many failures, he perfected his technique, and by the 1920s, perfectly round, lustrous cultured pearls began to flood the global market at a fraction of the cost of natural ones. The rarity and mystique that had made natural pearls so valuable evaporated almost overnight.

The second blow was the Great Depression. The Wall Street Crash of 1929 plunged the world into economic crisis, wiping out the market for luxury goods. Even those who could still afford them were no longer buying. The combination was catastrophic for Bahrain. The price of natural pearls plummeted. Merchants who had been fabulously wealthy one year found themselves bankrupt the next, their vast stocks of pearls now nearly worthless. The intricate web of credit and debt that had sustained the industry for centuries disintegrated. The 1930s were years of profound hardship, unemployment, and social unrest, as the single product that had defined the islands' economy for millennia became obsolete.

The collapse of the pearling industry was more than an economic disaster; it was a social revolution. The old power structure, dominated by the great *tawashin* families and the *nakhudas*, was shattered. Their source of wealth and influence had vanished, and with it, their ability to keep thousands of men locked in debt bondage. For the first time in generations, the divers were free from their inherited debts, but they were also utterly destitute, a massive unemployed workforce in an economy with no alternative to offer.

This social and economic vacuum coincided with a new era of British-led administrative reform, overseen by the ruler's adviser, Charles Belgrave, who had arrived in 1926. The demise of the old pearling elite allowed the state to centralize its authority in an unprecedented way. The crisis created both the urgent need and the political opportunity for modernization. But more importantly, just as one resource-based economy died, another was about to be born. In 1932, as dhows rotted on the shores and divers wondered how they would feed their families, engineers in the island's interior made a discovery. The unemployed men of the pearling industry, hardened by a life of immense physical labor, would soon form the first workforce for a new source of wealth, one that lay not in the shallow seas, but deep beneath the desert sands.

CHAPTER TWELVE: Black Gold: The Discovery of Oil and the Transformation of a Nation

The collapse was total. The intricate, centuries-old world of the pearl trade, which had been the engine of Bahrain's economy since antiquity, had not just declined; it had evaporated. The Japanese cultured pearl and the global financial crash of 1929 had delivered a knockout blow from which there was no recovery. By the early 1930s, the suqs of Manama were quiet, the great merchant houses of Muharraq were closing their ledgers on worthless assets, and thousands of unemployed divers, suddenly freed from a lifetime of debt but with no means to feed their families, faced a future of utter destitution. The islands, which had once been the glittering hub of a global luxury trade, were sliding into a deep and desperate poverty. It was in this atmosphere of impending ruin that a handful of prospectors, driven by a stubborn belief that another kind of treasure lay beneath the sand, began their work. Few could have imagined that their efforts would not just rescue the islands from bankruptcy, but would fundamentally remake every aspect of Bahraini life.

The idea of oil in Bahrain was not new, but it was far from popular. For years, the dominant geological wisdom, championed by the formidable Anglo-Persian Oil Company (APOC), held that the Arabian side of the Gulf was barren. APOC, which had struck oil in Persia in 1908 and effectively held a monopoly on British-backed exploration in the region, had conducted a cursory survey of Bahrain in the early 1920s and dismissed it. Their geologists saw the distinctive Jebel Dukhan, the "Mountain of Smoke" at the island's center, as an unpromising geological feature. The consensus in London was that the real prize lay in Persia and Mesopotamia, and that Bahrain was a distraction.

This professional skepticism, however, failed to deter a man of legendary persistence: a New Zealand-born mining engineer and adventurer named Major Frank Holmes. Holmes was not a geologist, but he had a prospector's intuition and an unshakeable belief that the same geological structures that held oil in Persia must extend across the Gulf. Having secured exploration options from various Gulf rulers in the 1920s, he spent years trudging through the financial districts of London, trying to convince British oil companies to invest in a Bahraini venture. He was met with polite indifference and outright dismissal. APOC, secure in its Persian fields and jealously guarding its regional dominance, had no interest in pursuing what its experts considered a geological fantasy. For Holmes, the British door was firmly shut.

Undeterred, Holmes turned his gaze across the Atlantic. The great American oil companies, flush with cash and eager to secure their own overseas reserves, were not bound by the geological dogmas of the British. In 1927, Holmes successfully pitched his Bahraini concession to Gulf Oil. The deal immediately hit a geopolitical roadblock. The British government, which controlled Bahrain's foreign affairs under the terms of its treaties, was deeply suspicious of American commercial encroachment into its sphere of influence. Whitehall insisted that the Bahrain concession could only be held by a British company. Since Gulf Oil had a stake in the Turkish Petroleum Company (the future Iraq Petroleum Company) which was bound by the "Red Line Agreement"—a pact that restricted its members from seeking independent oil concessions in much of the former Ottoman Empire—it was forced to sell its Bahraini option.

The option was snapped up by another American giant, the Standard Oil Company of California (Socal), which was not a party to the Red Line Agreement. Socal was willing to play by Britain's rules. To circumvent the nationality clause, they established a wholly-owned subsidiary in Canada, which as a part of the British Commonwealth, qualified as a British company. This new entity was given a name that would soon become synonymous with the modernization of Bahrain: the Bahrain Petroleum Company, or Bapco. After prolonged and complex negotiations involving the company, the ruler, Sheikh Hamad bin Isa Al Khalifa, and the British authorities, the final agreement was signed on December 2, 1930. Bapco was granted exclusive exploration and exploitation rights over the entire country for the next 55 years. In return, the ruler would receive a royalty for every ton of oil extracted. It was a standard colonial-era concession, but for a nearly bankrupt state, it was a lifeline.

With the legal hurdles cleared, the Americans arrived. In 1931, the quiet desert landscape of central Bahrain was transformed. A small team of American geologists and drillers, led by Fred Davies and Guy Williams, set up camp at the foot of the Jebel Dukhan. It was a scene of stark cultural contrast: seasoned oilmen from Texas and California, accustomed to a very different kind of frontier, now working in the intense summer heat alongside Bahraini laborers, many of whom were former pearl divers. They brought with them enormous drilling rigs, trucks, and a technical vocabulary that was entirely alien to the local population.

The chosen location for the first well was a spot on the northern flank of the Jebel Dukhan. The American drillers were confident. Their geological surveys had suggested that the Jebel was a large anticline, a dome-like structure perfect for trapping oil. On October 10, 1931, the drill bit of Jebel Dukhan Well No. 1 began its slow, grinding descent into the limestone rock. For months, the work continued, a noisy, greasy, and monotonous routine under the desert sun. Then, in the early morning of June 1, 1932, at a depth of 2,008 feet, the well blew. It was not a dramatic gusher of Hollywood fame, but a steady, controlled flow of crude oil. After years of Holmes's persistence and months of drilling, black gold had been struck. Bahrain had just become the first state on the Arab side of the Persian Gulf to find oil.

The initial reaction was one of cautious optimism. The flow rate was modest, around 400 barrels a day, but it was enough to prove that oil existed in commercial quantities. For Sheikh Hamad and his British adviser, Charles Belgrave, it was a moment of profound relief. The news electrified the small world of the international oil industry and sent shockwaves through the geological departments of its major players. The discovery in Bahrain fundamentally challenged the prevailing wisdom and proved that Arabia was not barren. It triggered a frantic new oil rush, with companies scrambling to secure concessions in the neighboring territories. The most significant consequence was that it encouraged Socal to redouble its efforts on the nearby mainland of Saudi Arabia, where just six years later, it would make one of the largest oil discoveries in human history.

For Bahrain, the transformation was immediate and profound. The first shipment of crude oil sailed from the newly constructed terminal at Sitra in 1934, a moment celebrated with a grand ceremony attended by the ruler and foreign dignitaries. The royalties began to flow into the state treasury, providing the government with a stable and substantial source of revenue for the first time in its history. Before oil, the ruler's income was derived from customs duties and taxes on the date palm gardens and the pearling industry—sources that were unpredictable and, in the case of pearling, had vanished completely. Oil revenue changed everything. It gave the state the financial power to act, to build, and to modernize.

The most visible sign of this new power was the creation of a modern infrastructure. Guided by Belgrave, the government embarked on a series of ambitious projects. A network of paved roads was built, connecting Manama to the far-flung villages. The Sheikh Hamad Causeway, a landmark piece of engineering, was completed in 1942, linking the main island of Bahrain with the island of Muharraq, the old pearling capital. For the first time, the two main centers of the country were connected by land, ending Muharraq's historic isolation. Electricity and telephone services were introduced, slowly transforming the fabric of urban life.

The oil industry itself became the primary engine of this change. Bapco was not just an oil company; it was a state within a state, building its own world in the middle of the island. It constructed a large-scale refinery, which began operations in 1936 and quickly became one of the most important industrial facilities in the entire region. To house its growing workforce, it built a new town, Awali. Designed and run on American lines, Awali was an insulated expatriate enclave, a slice of suburbia transplanted into the Arabian desert, complete with air-conditioned houses, a swimming pool, a cinema, and a hospital. It stood in stark contrast to the traditional coral-stone and palm-frond houses of the Bahraini villages, a constant and visible reminder of the foreign presence that was driving the country's modernization.

The greatest social impact was on the labor force. The collapse of the pearling industry had created a vast pool of unemployed men. Bapco provided the alternative. Thousands of former divers, haulers, and sailors traded the precarious, seasonal, debt-ridden life on a dhow for the regimented, wage-earning life of an industrial worker. The transition was not always easy. The new work involved regular hours, shift work, and the unfamiliar discipline of the factory floor. But it also offered a steady cash wage, freeing workers from the cycles of debt that had defined the pearling economy. This shift from a credit-based, semi-feudal system to a modern, cash-based economy was one of the most fundamental social changes brought by the discovery of oil.

The newfound oil wealth also funded the creation of a welfare state. While the first modern schools and a small clinic had been established before the oil era, the new revenues allowed for a massive expansion of public services. A comprehensive system of state education was developed, offering free schooling to both boys and girls, a progressive step for the time and place. In 1940, the government opened the Naim Hospital (later renamed Salmaniya Medical Complex), the first large, modern public hospital, offering free healthcare to all citizens. These investments in education and health would have a profound long-term impact, creating a skilled and educated local workforce that would become a hallmark of Bahrain's development.

The strategic importance of Bahrain's oil, and particularly its refinery, became starkly clear during the Second World War. As a secure source of fuel for the Royal Navy and Allied forces in the Middle East and Asia, the Bapco refinery was a significant strategic asset. Its importance was not lost on the Axis powers. On the night of October 19, 1940, in one of the more unusual episodes of the war, long-range bombers of the Italian Royal Air Force, flying all the way from bases on the Greek island of Rhodes, carried out a raid on Bahrain. Their primary target was the refinery. The raid itself was largely a failure; most of the bombs fell harmlessly in the desert, and the damage to the oil installations was minimal. However, it was a dramatic demonstration that Bahrain's newfound resource had placed it squarely on the map of global conflict.

After the war, the pace of change only accelerated. Oil production increased, and the refinery was expanded to process crude oil piped in from the newly developed fields in Saudi Arabia via an undersea pipeline, solidifying Bahrain's position as a major refining and export center. The revenues pouring into the state coffers continued to fund the expansion of the modern state. By the 1950s, a generation had come of age that had no memory of the pearling era. Their world was one of oil derricks, refineries, regular wages, and state-funded schools.

This transformation, however, was not without its tensions. The creation of a large industrial working class, concentrated in a single industry run by a foreign company, created the perfect conditions for new political ideas and new forms of organization to take root. The stark disparity between the lifestyles of the expatriate managers in Awali and the Bahraini workers in their villages bred resentment. The very process of education that the oil wealth had funded was creating a new generation of politically aware Bahrainis who were beginning to question the colonial nature of the political system and demand a greater say in the running of their country. The black gold that had rescued Bahrain from economic collapse had also unleashed powerful new social and political forces. It had built a modern state, but in doing so, it had also laid the groundwork for the winds of change that would sweep through the nation in the decades to come.

CHAPTER THIRTEEN: The Winds of Change: Nationalism and the Path to Independence

The oil that flowed from Jebel Dukhan Well No. 1 did more than just fill the state's coffers; it irrigated the seeds of a new political consciousness. The Bahrain that emerged from the Second World War was a nation fundamentally altered. A generation had grown up with access to state-funded schools, not just the traditional Quranic ones. Thousands of men had traded the capricious rhythms of the pearling dhow for the regimented shifts of the Bapco refinery. A new middle class of clerks, teachers, and small businessmen had emerged, and a large, concentrated industrial working class had been forged. These groups were literate, connected, and increasingly aware of the vast political currents sweeping the world beyond their shores. The old order—a ruling sheikh advised by a seemingly permanent British official, Charles Belgrave, and protected by the long shadow of the British Empire—began to seem less like a natural state of affairs and more like a political arrangement that could, and perhaps should, be challenged.

The new ideas arrived, as they so often do, through the air. In the coffee houses of Manama and the workers' camps near the refinery, men would huddle around crackling radios, tuning in to the powerful broadcasts of *Sawt al-Arab*, the "Voice of the Arabs," from Cairo. The charismatic voice of Egyptian President Gamal Abdel Nasser filled the night, speaking a potent new language of pan-Arab nationalism, anti-imperialism, and social justice. His message resonated deeply in Bahrain, where the most powerful corporation was American, the ultimate political authority was British, and the chief administrator, Belgrave, was an Englishman who had been the power behind the throne since before most people were born. Nasser's speeches made the abstract concept of foreign domination feel personal and immediate.

This growing political awareness first found its voice not in the salons of the educated elite, but in the oil fields. The Bapco workforce, a mix of Bahrainis, other Arabs, Persians, and South Asians, was a microcosm of the country's diverse society, and a natural incubator for collective action. A series of strikes in 1938 and 1943, though primarily focused on wages and working conditions, were early signs of a workforce learning to organize and assert its demands. The stark contrast between the segregated, air-conditioned luxury of the American town of Awali and the simple living conditions of the local workers was a daily, visible reminder of the inequalities of the new oil economy. The workers were not just demanding better pay; they were demanding dignity and an end to a system that treated them as second-class citizens in their own country.

These simmering discontents finally coalesced in the mid-1950s into the most significant political movement in Bahrain's modern history. In 1954, following a series of sectarian disputes that many believed were stoked by the authorities to divide the populace, a group of eight prominent men—four Sunni and four Shia—came together to form the Committee of National Union, which was soon renamed the National Union Committee (NUC). Led by charismatic figures like the intellectual Abdul Rahman Al-Baker and the eloquent writer Abdulaziz Al-Shamlan, the NUC was a broad-based, cross-sectarian nationalist movement. It was not a revolutionary cabal seeking to overthrow the ruler, Sheikh Salman bin Hamad Al Khalifa, but a reformist movement with a clear and modernizing agenda.

Their demands were spelled out in petitions and proclaimed at mass rallies that drew enormous crowds. They called for an end to British influence and the dismissal of Charles Belgrave, whom they saw as the symbol of colonial rule. They demanded a legislative council elected by the people to create laws and hold the government accountable. They insisted on the codification of laws and the establishment of a unified court system that would end the parallel jurisdiction of the British Agency courts, which held sway over foreigners. Finally, they called for the right to form trade unions to protect the new working class. It was a vision of a modern, constitutional state, a radical departure from the autocratic, paternalistic system that had governed the islands for decades.

The NUC's main weapon was the general strike. In July 1954 and again in March 1956, the committee brought the country to a standstill. The Bapco refinery shut down, the docks fell silent, and the suqs of Manama and Muharraq closed their doors. The strikes were a stunning demonstration of the committee's popular support and its ability to mobilize the entire nation. The authorities were shaken. Sheikh Salman and Belgrave initially tried to defuse the situation through negotiation, creating their own reform committees and offering concessions. But the nationalists, sensing their strength, held firm. They were not interested in cosmetic changes; they wanted a fundamental shift in the distribution of political power.

The standoff came to a head in the autumn of 1956. The Suez Crisis, in which Britain, France, and Israel invaded Egypt following Nasser's nationalization of the Suez Canal, sent a tidal wave of anti-British fury across the Arab world. In Bahrain, the NUC organized massive demonstrations in support of Egypt. The protests turned into riots, and government buildings were attacked. For the British, this was no longer a local labor dispute or a call for reform; it was a direct challenge to the stability of a key strategic asset in the Persian Gulf at a moment of intense regional crisis. The patience of the British Political Resident, Sir Bernard Burrows, ran out. He saw the NUC as a vehicle for Nasser's influence and a threat to British interests.

The crackdown was swift. With British backing, Sheikh Salman declared a state of emergency. In November 1956, the leaders of the NUC—Al-Baker, Al-Shamlan, and three others—were arrested. They were charged with attempting to overthrow the government and fomenting unrest. After a hastily arranged trial, they were sentenced to long prison terms. To ensure they could not become martyrs on home soil, the British flew them out of Bahrain to a place of remote imperial exile: the tiny, windswept island of St. Helena in the South Atlantic, the same island where Napoleon

Bonaparte had been imprisoned more than a century earlier. The message was clear: open political dissent would not be tolerated.

The NUC was crushed, but its ghost lingered. The movement had failed in its ultimate objectives, but it had irrevocably changed the political landscape. It had demonstrated the power of popular mobilization and had articulated a set of national aspirations that would not go away. It also made Charles Belgrave's position untenable. Having been the central target of the nationalists' anger, his continued presence was seen by both Bahrainis and the British Foreign Office as an obstacle to stability. In 1957, after thirty-one years as the most powerful man in Bahrain, Belgrave quietly "retired" and left the island for good. His departure was a quiet victory for the movement he had helped to suppress.

The decade that followed was one of enforced political tranquility. With the nationalist leaders in exile and public political activity banned, the country entered a period of quiet consolidation under a new ruler, Sheikh Isa bin Salman Al Khalifa, who ascended in 1961 upon the death of his father. While political expression was suppressed, the process of administrative modernization, which the NUC had demanded, continued apace. Sheikh Isa, a pragmatic and forward-looking ruler, established the framework of a modern government. An Administrative Council was created to oversee the expanding state bureaucracy, and this was later transformed into the State Council, a body that functioned as a proto-cabinet, with members of the Al Khalifa family and prominent commoners appointed to head various government departments. Bahrain was building the institutions of a state, even as the question of its ultimate sovereignty remained unresolved.

The question was forced into the open not by events in Manama, but by a bombshell announcement from London. In January 1968, the British Labour government of Prime Minister Harold Wilson, wrestling with a severe economic crisis at home, declared that it would withdraw all of its military forces from the major bases "East of Suez" by the end of 1971. For over a century, the rulers of Bahrain had outsourced their defense and foreign policy to the British Crown. The *Pax Britannica* had been the defining reality of their political existence, protecting them from ambitious neighbors and internal rivals. Now, suddenly, the protector was leaving. The news was met with a mixture of excitement and profound anxiety throughout the Gulf. The British withdrawal would create a dangerous power vacuum, and Bahrain, a small and wealthy archipelago, would be dangerously exposed.

Two major obstacles stood on the path to a smooth transition to independence. The first was the long-standing and vociferously argued claim to sovereignty over Bahrain by its powerful neighbor, Iran. The Shah of Iran, Mohammad Reza Pahlavi, considered Bahrain historically part of the Persian Empire and often referred to it as his country's "14th province." This claim, though never enforced by military action, was a constant source of diplomatic tension and a potential justification for an Iranian takeover once the British departed. The second obstacle was Britain's own preferred exit strategy. London hoped to bundle its nine Gulf protectorates—Bahrain, Qatar, and the seven Trucial States that would become the United Arab Emirates—into a single federation. The idea was to create a larger, more viable state that could better defend itself in a turbulent region.

Negotiations for the federation began, but they quickly bogged down. Bahrain was in a very different position from the other sheikhdoms. It was more populous, more economically developed, had a longer history of administrative modernization, and a more politically sophisticated population. In any federation based on population, Bahrain would naturally be the dominant partner, a prospect that worried the other rulers. For Bahrain, being yoked to less-developed states was seen by many as a step backward. After two years of fruitless negotiations, it became clear that the federation was not a viable path for Bahrain.

This left the thorny issue of the Iranian claim. Direct confrontation was unthinkable, and a compromise seemed impossible. The solution, when it came, was a masterpiece of face-saving diplomacy. The Shah, under quiet pressure from Britain and the United States, who wanted a stable, pro-Western Gulf after the British withdrawal, agreed to renounce his claim, but he could not be seen to simply surrender it. He needed a way to bow to the inevitable without losing face. The agreed-upon mechanism was to invite the United Nations to send a special mission to Bahrain to "ascertain the wishes of the people."

In April 1970, a small UN team led by an Italian diplomat, Vittorio Winspeare-Guicciardi, arrived in Manama. This was not a referendum or an election. Instead, over a period of two weeks, Winspeare-Guicciardi and his team conducted an exhaustive series of interviews. They met with the leaders of hundreds of organizations: sporting clubs, cultural societies, religious groups, village elders, business associations, and professional bodies. They sought out a representative cross-section of Bahraini society and asked them one fundamental question about their political future.

The mission's findings, submitted to the UN Secretary-General, were unequivocal. The report concluded that the "overwhelming majority of the people of Bahrain wish to gain recognition of their identity in a fully independent and sovereign State free to decide for itself its relations with other States." The language was carefully chosen, but the meaning was unmistakable. On May 11, 1970, the United Nations Security Council unanimously endorsed the report. A few days later, the Iranian parliament formally accepted the result and renounced its centuries-old claim. The final diplomatic hurdle had been cleared.

With the federation idea abandoned and the Iranian claim resolved, the way forward was clear. The last year of British protection was spent finalizing the details of the transition. New treaties of friendship were drafted to replace the old protectorate agreements. On August 15, 1971, Sheikh Isa bin Salman Al Khalifa went on the radio and formally declared the full independence of the State of Bahrain. After 150 years, the era of the *Pax Britannica* was over. The winds of change that had begun to blow in the post-war years had finally carried the island nation to its destination as a sovereign member of the international community.

CHAPTER FOURTEEN: Building a Modern State: The Early Years of Independence (1971-1981)

On the fifteenth of August 1971, the Union Jack was lowered for the last time, bringing 150 years of British protection to a quiet and unceremonious end. For the first time in centuries, Bahrain was the master of its own destiny. The sense of national pride was immense, but it was tempered by a sober understanding of the challenges ahead. A new state had to be built, not just in name, but in practice. Sheikh Isa bin Salman Al Khalifa, the ruler, formally shed the title of *Hakim* for the grander, more modern title of Amir. The old State Council was dissolved and replaced by a formal Council of Ministers, a cabinet to run the machinery of a sovereign government. The work of turning an oil-rich protectorate into a viable nation-state began at once.

The first order of business was to claim Bahrain's seat on the world stage. Within a month, the country had joined the United Nations and the Arab League, anchoring its identity in both the international community and the Arab world. A Ministry of Foreign Affairs was established to manage the country's external relations, a task that had been handled by British officials for generations. Embassies were opened, and diplomats dispatched. A national military, the Bahrain Defence Force (BDF), was formally established to take over the responsibility for national security, a role previously filled by the British military. Domestically, a new currency was issued, and the national flag, once a symbol of a ruling family, became the emblem of a sovereign people. These were the essential building blocks of statehood, the tangible proofs that Bahrain was no longer a dependency but a nation in its own right.

Yet, the most ambitious and ultimately most contentious project of this first decade was the creation of a political framework for the new state. Fulfilling a promise made on the eve of independence, the Amir decreed that a constitution would be written. In December 1972, Bahrain held its first-ever national election, choosing twenty-two delegates to a Constituent Assembly. This body, which also included appointed government ministers and members of the ruling family, was tasked with drafting the nation's founding charter. The electorate was restricted to native-born male citizens over the age of twenty, but it was nonetheless a momentous step. After months of vigorous debate, the assembly produced the Constitution of 1973, a remarkably progressive document for its time and place. It declared Bahrain a constitutional monarchy, guaranteed basic freedoms, and, most importantly, vested legislative power in a unicameral, elected parliament to be called the National Assembly.

In December 1973, the country went to the polls again, this time to elect thirty members to the new National Assembly. The results produced a vibrant, fractious, and deeply ideological body. The chamber was a cross-section of Bahraini society and its political currents. One bloc consisted of leftists and Arab nationalists, heirs to the spirit of the 1950s National Union Committee. Another was a "Religious Bloc" of Shia Islamists who sought a greater role for religion in public life. A third, dubbed the "People's Bloc," was a collection of independent merchants and notables. With government ministers also sitting in the chamber as ex-officio members, the stage was set for a political drama the likes of which Bahrain had never seen.

The Assembly quickly became a forum for passionate debate and a major check on the government's power. Its members questioned ministers, scrutinized the budget, and challenged government policy with a vigor that surprised many. They debated everything from the price of fish to the nation's foreign policy. This experiment in parliamentary democracy proved to be short-lived. A fundamental clash soon emerged between a government accustomed to ruling by decree and an assembly determined to exercise its constitutional powers to the fullest. The flashpoint was a piece of legislation proposed by the government in 1974: the State Security Law. This law gave the Ministry of Interior sweeping powers to arrest and detain individuals deemed a threat to national security for up to three years without trial.

To many members of the Assembly, the law was a direct assault on the personal freedoms guaranteed by the new constitution. They saw it as a tool to crush dissent and roll back the country's political progress. The government, on the other hand, argued it was a necessary measure to combat subversion and maintain stability in a volatile region. The debate was fierce and irreconcilable. Another major point of friction was the government's decision to grant the United States Navy the use of the former British naval base at Juffair. For the leftist and nationalist members of the Assembly, allowing a Western military presence on Bahraini soil was a betrayal of the very independence they had just gained. The Assembly and the government were in a state of perpetual gridlock.

In August 1975, the experiment came to an abrupt end. Citing the Assembly's refusal to cooperate with the government, the Amir, Sheikh Isa, exercised his constitutional right to dissolve the body. The constitution stipulated that new elections must be held within two months, but a subsequent Amiri decree postponed them indefinitely. The National Assembly would not meet again for twenty-seven years. The State Security Law was implemented by decree, and the era of parliamentary politics was over. The brief, two-year lifespan of the National Assembly left a complex legacy. For some, it was a cautionary tale of a political experiment that went too far, too fast, threatening to destabilize the new state. For others, it was a golden age of free expression and political participation, a dream of constitutional government that was prematurely extinguished.

With the political question settled by decree, the government turned its full attention to economic and social construction. The timing could not have been better. The 1973 Arab-Israeli War and the subsequent OPEC oil embargo led to a massive surge in global oil prices. The resulting tsunami of petrodollars that washed over the Gulf transformed the region's economic landscape. Bahrain, though a modest oil producer, was perfectly positioned to benefit.

The government used this windfall to accelerate its ambitious development plans, focusing on heavy industry and infrastructure. The Aluminium Bahrain (Alba) smelter, which had opened just before independence, was significantly expanded, becoming one of the largest in the world and the cornerstone of a new non-oil industrial sector. To service the massive oil tankers that plied the Gulf's waters, the Arab Shipbuilding and Repair Yard (ASRY) dry dock was constructed, opening in 1977 and cementing Bahrain's status as a key maritime service hub.

The most transformative economic decision of the decade, however, was a stroke of strategic brilliance. In 1975, as civil war tore apart the Lebanese capital of Beirut, the Middle East's traditional financial center, Bahrain saw an opportunity. The Bahrain Monetary Agency, the country's new central bank, invited international banks to establish "Offshore Banking Units" (OBUs) on the island. These OBUs were offered an attractive package: they were exempt from taxes, reserve requirements, and foreign exchange controls, in return for an annual license fee and a promise not to deal in the local currency or with the domestic market. The response was overwhelming. Major international banks, fleeing the chaos of Beirut and looking for a safe and stable hub to manage the region's vast new oil wealth, flocked to Manama. In a few short years, Bahrain became the undisputed financial capital of the Gulf, a crucial node in the global flow of petrodollars.

This new wealth funded a dramatic expansion of the welfare state. The government poured money into education, healthcare, electricity, and water, extending modern services to every corner of the country. The most visible legacy of this era is the vast public housing program. New towns, most notably the sprawling and meticulously planned Isa Town, were constructed to provide modern, subsidized housing for thousands of Bahraini families, replacing traditional palm-frond houses with concrete villas and apartment blocks. This investment in human capital and social infrastructure dramatically raised the standard of living and created a well-educated and relatively healthy population, which would become one of the country's greatest assets.

In foreign policy, the decade was a delicate balancing act. Without the security blanket of the British treaty, Bahrain had to navigate a dangerous neighborhood on its own. The cornerstone of its new foreign policy was a deep and abiding strategic alliance with its giant neighbor, Saudi Arabia. This relationship provided a crucial security guarantee and political backing. Pragmatism also guided its relationship with the West. The departure of the Royal Navy was almost immediately followed by an agreement with the United States to allow its small Middle East Force to use naval facilities at Juffair. This decision provided another layer of security but was deeply controversial among Arab nationalists, both at home and abroad.

As the decade drew to a close, the regional landscape shifted seismically. In 1979, the Iranian Revolution replaced the Shah's monarchy, a historical rival but also a predictable partner, with a revolutionary Islamic Republic. The new regime in Tehran, led by Ayatollah Khomeini, declared its intention to export its revolution, and its rhetoric revived old anxieties. Radio broadcasts from Iran began calling for the overthrow of the Gulf monarchies, and Bahrain, with its majority Shia population, was seen as particularly vulnerable. The revolution injected a new and potent strain of political Islam into the region, exacerbating sectarian tensions that had long simmered beneath the surface.

The sense of external threat intensified dramatically in September 1980, when Iraq invaded Iran, plunging the Gulf into a long and brutal war. The conflict between two of the region's most powerful states created a new and alarming level of instability. For the small states of the Arabian Peninsula, suddenly living in the shadow of a major regional war, the need for collective security became paramount. This shared sense of vulnerability was the driving force behind a new regional alliance. In May 1981, the leaders of Bahrain, Saudi Arabia, Kuwait, Qatar, the United Arab Emirates, and Oman met in Abu Dhabi to sign the charter establishing the Gulf Cooperation Council (GCC). Created as a political and economic alliance to foster integration and coordination, its unstated primary purpose was collective security in the face of the new dangers emanating from Iran and the war raging to the north.

As its first decade of independence concluded, Bahrain had successfully built the foundations of a modern state and a diversified economy, but it had also entered a new era of regional uncertainty, binding its future ever more tightly to that of its Gulf neighbors.

CHAPTER FIFTEEN: Navigating Regional Conflicts: The Iran-Iraq War and Gulf Tensions

The first decade of Bahrain's independence had been a whirlwind of state-building, economic transformation, and a brief, heady experiment with parliamentary democracy. As the 1980s dawned, however, the focus shifted dramatically from the internal to the external. The neighbourhood had become a far more dangerous place. The Iranian Revolution of 1979 had replaced a predictable, if sometimes difficult, monarchy with a revolutionary theocracy whose stated goal was to export its ideology across the region. A year later, Iraq's invasion of Iran plunged the Gulf into a long and brutal war, its shockwaves felt in every capital from Muscat to Kuwait City. For the newly sovereign state of Bahrain, the decade would be a long and tense exercise in navigating the treacherous currents of regional conflict, a period where national security became the government's paramount concern and strategic alliances were forged in the crucible of shared threat.

The ideological challenge from Tehran was felt with particular acuteness in Manama. The new Iranian regime's revolutionary rhetoric, broadcast powerfully across the Gulf in Arabic, resonated with a segment of Bahrain's majority Shia population who felt marginalized from the country's political and economic power structures. Ayatollah Khomeini's message was not just religious; it was profoundly political, calling for the overthrow of the Gulf's monarchies, which he branded as corrupt, un-Islamic, and puppets of the West. This rhetoric revived old anxieties about Persian expansionism, now cloaked in the mantle of revolutionary Islam. For the government of Bahrain, the threat was not a hypothetical foreign policy problem; it was an immediate and direct challenge to its legitimacy and stability.

The challenge took concrete form with shocking speed. In the early hours of December 13, 1981, Bahraini security forces began a series of coordinated raids, arresting a group of men who were allegedly in the final stages of plotting a coup d'état. The plot was audacious. The plan, according to the government, was for the conspirators to seize key government buildings and the state radio station during the national day celebrations on December 16th, assassinate government officials, and proclaim an Islamic republic. It was a scenario seemingly ripped from the headlines of the Iranian Revolution itself. The group behind the plot was a shadowy organization called the Islamic Front for the Liberation of Bahrain (IFLB), an organization founded in Iran in 1979 and composed mainly of Bahraini Shia exiles who had studied in religious seminaries in Najaf and Qom.

The subsequent investigation uncovered what the government described as a clear case of Iranian state sponsorship. The seventy-three men arrested—a mix of Bahrainis, Saudis, Kuwaitis, and Omanis—had allegedly received military training in camps in Iran. Their leader was an Iranian-based cleric, Hojjat al-Islam Hadi al-Mudarri, who had been an official in the new revolutionary government. The cache of weapons seized was reported to have been smuggled into the country by sea from Iran. For Bahrain and its newly formed Gulf Cooperation Council (GCC) partners, the plot was irrefutable proof of Tehran's hostile intentions. Iran vehemently denied any involvement, dismissing the accusations as a pretext for a crackdown on the Shia population. Whatever the precise level of official Iranian direction, the coup attempt was a profound shock to the system. It transformed the ideological threat from Tehran into a clear and present danger, shattering any lingering hopes that the revolution could be contained within Iran's borders.

The immediate aftermath was a dramatic tightening of domestic security. The State Security Law of 1974, which had been the source of such conflict during the brief parliamentary era, now became the primary legal tool for the state. A new wave of arrests followed, targeting individuals suspected of sympathizing with the plotters or with the revolutionary message from Iran. The government also began to scrutinize the activities of religious centers and charitable societies more closely. The coup plot had a chilling effect on the country's political atmosphere, creating a climate of suspicion and raising sectarian tensions to a level not seen in decades. It also reinforced the government's conviction that political openness was a luxury the state could not afford in such a perilous security environment.

The failed coup had an equally profound impact on foreign policy. It galvanized the fledgling GCC, which had been founded just seven months earlier. The shared threat gave the new organization an urgent sense of purpose. In the weeks following the discovery of the plot, the GCC interior ministers rushed to sign a comprehensive internal security pact, facilitating intelligence sharing and extradition among the member states. The dream of economic and social integration was now firmly secondary to the immediate necessity of collective security. Bahrain, having been the first target, became a vocal advocate for deeper security cooperation. The incident provided the impetus for the creation of the GCC's joint military arm, the Peninsula Shield Force, a rapid deployment force established in 1984 to deter and respond to external aggression against any member state. For Bahrain, the alliance with its Gulf neighbors, and particularly with the regional heavyweight Saudi Arabia, was no longer just a policy choice; it was the cornerstone of its national survival.

This strategic alignment was given monumental form in concrete and steel. On November 26, 1986, King Fahd of Saudi Arabia and Sheikh Isa bin Salman Al Khalifa met in the middle of a newly constructed bridge to officially inaugurate the King Fahd Causeway. The 25-kilometer (16-mile) chain of bridges and causeways was a breathtaking feat of engineering, physically linking the island of Bahrain to the Arabian mainland for the first time in history. The project, financed almost entirely by Saudi Arabia at a cost of over one billion dollars, was far more than an infrastructure project. It was the ultimate symbol of the strategic bond between the two countries. While it brought immense economic benefits, facilitating trade and tourism, its primary rationale was strategic. The causeway ensured that, in the event of a crisis, Bahrain could be rapidly reinforced by its powerful ally. It was a permanent, physical guarantee against external aggression and a clear message to Tehran that Bahrain was not alone.

Throughout these years, the dominant reality of the region was the grinding, bloody stalemate of the Iran-Iraq War. From its outbreak in September 1980 until the ceasefire in August 1988, the conflict cast a long shadow over the Gulf. Officially, Bahrain, like its GCC partners, maintained a position of neutrality. In practice, however, its sympathies and support lay firmly with Iraq. This was not due to any great affection for Saddam Hussein's regime, but to a cold strategic calculation. The GCC states saw Iraq as a vital bulwark, the "eastern flank of the Arab world," holding the line against the expansionist ambitions of revolutionary Iran. A victory for Iran was seen as an existential threat that would destabilize the entire region and potentially lead to the collapse of the Gulf monarchies.

Consequently, Bahrain became part of a massive logistical and financial effort to prop up the Iraqi war machine. The Gulf states poured tens of billions of dollars in loans and grants into Baghdad. Bahrain's ports and financial institutions played a crucial role in this effort. With Iraq's own Gulf ports closed by the fighting, goods and military supplies destined for the Iraqi front were often offloaded in GCC ports and transported overland. Bahrain's Offshore Banking Units, which had made it the region's financial hub, were instrumental in managing the vast financial transactions that sustained the Iraqi economy through eight years of war.

As the war dragged on, it became increasingly dangerous for those on its periphery. In 1984, the conflict escalated into a new and perilous phase known as the "Tanker War." Both Iran and Iraq began attacking each other's oil tankers and merchant shipping in the Gulf in an attempt to cripple their opponent's economy. Soon, the attacks expanded to include neutral vessels trading with either side. The waters of the Gulf, Bahrain's lifeline to the world, became a war zone. Dozens of ships were hit by Iraqi Exocet missiles or Iranian Silkworm missiles and gunboats. Insurance premiums for shipping in the Gulf skyrocketed. For Bahrain, a state utterly dependent on maritime trade, the Tanker War was a direct threat to its economic stability. The regular explosions and plumes of smoke on the horizon were a constant, unnerving reminder of the major conflict raging just a few hundred kilometers to the north.

The situation reached a crisis point in 1986-87, as Iranian attacks on Kuwaiti shipping intensified. In a move to protect its fleet, Kuwait requested that its tankers be re-registered under the American flag, allowing them to be escorted by the United States Navy. This led to a massive increase in the Western naval presence in the Gulf. The small American naval facility in Juffair, which had been a quiet backwater for years, was suddenly thrust into a central role as a key logistical hub for the US fleet engaged in Operation Earnest Will, the convoy protection mission. The waters around Bahrain teemed with American warships, minesweepers, and helicopters. This reliance on an external protector was a pragmatic necessity, but it was also a source of political unease, exposing the GCC's inability to guarantee its own maritime security and making Bahrain a potential target in any wider confrontation between the US and Iran. The risks became terrifyingly real in May 1987, when an Iraqi jet fighter mistakenly fired two missiles into the side of the USS Stark, an American frigate patrolling near Bahrain, killing 37 sailors. The incident, though a case of mistaken identity, highlighted the extreme volatility of the conflict and the danger of operating in the Gulf's crowded and trigger-happy environment.

The long war of attrition finally ground to a halt in August 1988, when a battered and exhausted Iran accepted a UN-brokered ceasefire. A collective sigh of relief went through the Gulf. For Bahrain, the end of the war brought an end to eight years of living on a knife's edge. The direct threat of military escalation receded, and the waters of the Gulf became safe for shipping once more. The decade of navigating regional conflict had been a sobering experience. It had forced Bahrain to rapidly mature its foreign and security policies, binding it into a tight regional alliance through the GCC and a deeper, if more informal, security relationship with the West. The country had weathered the storm, its sovereignty intact and its economy surprisingly resilient. The external threats had, in a sense, forged a stronger and more pragmatic state. But the pressures of the decade had also left their mark internally, suppressing political life and exacerbating sectarian divisions that would re-emerge in the decade to come. The peace that settled over the Gulf in 1988 would prove to be tragically short-lived. The ally that Bahrain and its neighbors had spent a decade and a fortune supporting would, in just two years, become the region's next great threat.

CHAPTER SIXTEEN: The 1990s Uprising: Demands for Political Reform

The end of the Iran-Iraq War in 1988 brought a collective sigh of relief across the Gulf, but the peace it heralded was fleeting. Just two years later, the region was plunged into a new and even more alarming crisis when Saddam Hussein's Iraqi forces invaded and occupied Kuwait. For Bahrain, the 1991 Gulf War was a moment of acute danger and profound strategic importance. The island became a crucial air and naval base for the US-led coalition assembled to liberate Kuwait. Bahraini pilots flew combat missions over Iraq, and the country braced for retaliation, with three Iraqi Scud missiles being fired in its direction. One landed, causing no casualties, but it was a stark reminder of the country's vulnerability.

The swift and successful liberation of Kuwait, framed by the international community as a defense of sovereignty and international law, had an unintended consequence. It uncorked a new wave of political expectation across the region. If Western powers were willing to go to war to restore the legitimate ruler of Kuwait, many in the Arab world began to ask, why were they not equally supportive of citizens seeking greater political rights from their own rulers? In Bahrain, this question fell on fertile ground, watered by grievances that had been simmering for nearly two decades. The memory of the short-lived elected parliament of 1973 was still alive, and its dissolution in 1975 remained the country's great unanswered political question.

The political climate of the early 1990s was one of quiet but deep-seated frustration. Political parties were banned, and public dissent was effectively criminalized by the sweeping provisions of the 1974 State Security Law. This law granted the Ministry of Interior the power to arrest and imprison individuals for up to three years without trial for a wide range of vaguely defined offenses, from threatening state security to disseminating "subversive propaganda." It had created a climate of fear, particularly within the country's Shia majority, who felt they were disproportionately targeted.

Economic pressures added another layer of discontent. A downturn in oil prices in the late 1980s had strained the state's budget, and unemployment was a growing problem, particularly among young people entering the workforce. There was a widespread perception, especially within the Shia community, of systemic discrimination in hiring for desirable public sector jobs, particularly in the military and security services, which were dominated by Sunnis and non-Bahraini recruits. This sense of being excluded from both the political and economic life of the nation created a wellspring of resentment that was waiting for a channel of expression.

That channel began to form not on the streets, but through the careful drafting of petitions. In 1992, a group of 280 prominent citizens, a cross-section of society including secularists, leftists, and Islamists, both Sunni and Shia, and several members of the dissolved 1973 parliament, signed what became known as the "Elite Petition." In carefully respectful language, it called on the Amir, Sheikh Isa bin Salman Al Khalifa, to restore the 1973 constitution and reinstate the elected National Assembly. The government's response was to create a thirty-member appointed "Shura Council," or Consultative Council, tasked with commenting on government legislation. For the petitioners, this was a wholly inadequate substitute for a genuinely representative parliament, a body with no legislative power that only highlighted the democratic deficit they sought to address.

This polite but firm rejection spurred the opposition to broaden its campaign. In October 1994, a second, more ambitious petition was launched. Known as the "Popular Petition," it reiterated the demands of the first but was circulated widely among the general public. Organizers claimed to have gathered over 20,000 signatures, a significant number in a small country. This time, the government did not engage. The petition was ignored, and the atmosphere grew tense. The long-suppressed political frustrations were about to erupt into open conflict.

The spark came from an unlikely source: a charity marathon. In November 1994, hundreds of Shia villagers protested the route of the marathon, which passed through their communities, objecting to what they considered the immodest dress of some of the female runners. Scuffles broke out, stones were reportedly thrown, and the security forces moved in, making a number of arrests. In the following days, the government arrested a popular young Shia cleric, Sheikh Ali Salman, accusing him of inciting the incident.

The arrest of Sheikh Salman was the breaking point. Widespread protests demanding his release erupted in Manama and the surrounding Shia villages. The government responded with force, deploying riot police who used tear gas and rubber bullets to disperse the crowds. The cycle of the uprising had begun: a protest would be met with a harsh security response, leading to injuries or arrests. The funerals of those killed or the gatherings to protest the arrests would then become the catalyst for the next demonstration. What had started as a demand for constitutional reform had morphed into a sustained, low-level conflict that would grip the country for the next five years.

The uprising was a disjointed and largely leaderless movement in its day-to-day expression, but it had a clear spiritual and political guide. Sheikh Abdulamir al-Jamri, a respected senior Shia cleric and former member of the 1973 parliament, emerged as the public face and leading voice of the opposition. A skilled orator, Sheikh al-Jamri's Friday sermons became the primary vehicle for articulating the movement's demands and galvanizing its supporters. He consistently framed the struggle in peaceful, political terms, calling for the restoration of the constitution and an end to human rights abuses. Working alongside him were other key figures, including Abdulwahab Hussain and Hassan Mushaima, who helped to organize the disparate strands of the opposition. The movement also had an external wing, most notably the London-based Bahrain Freedom Movement (BFM), led by Said al-Shehabi, which used its website, "The Voice of Bahrain," to publicize the opposition's cause and report on events that were largely ignored by the state-controlled media at home.

The government's response was uncompromising. Led by the long-serving Prime Minister, Sheikh Khalifa bin Salman Al Khalifa, and the Ministry of Interior, the state viewed the uprising not as a legitimate call for reform, but as a violent, sectarian, and foreign-inspired threat to national security. The security forces, headed by the British-born Director of Security and Intelligence, Ian Henderson, were given a free hand to crush the unrest.

The tactics used were systematic. Night raids on the homes of suspected activists in the Shia villages became commonplace. Mass arrests followed every major protest, with human rights groups estimating that several thousand people were detained over the course of the uprising, often held for long periods without charge or trial under the provisions of the State Security Law. Allegations of systematic torture and ill-treatment of detainees were rampant. Reports from groups like Amnesty International and Human Rights Watch documented numerous cases of physical and psychological abuse, and several detainees died in custody under suspicious circumstances.

The government also used forced exile as a weapon. In January 1995, Sheikh Ali Salman and other opposition leaders were deported. Sheikh al-Jamri himself was placed under house arrest and then imprisoned in April 1995. He was briefly released in September after a rumoured deal with the government to calm the streets, but when the authorities denied any such agreement had been made, the protests resumed with renewed intensity. In January 1996, Sheikh al-Jamri was arrested again, along with his senior aides. This time he would remain in prison for years.

While the opposition insisted its methods were primarily peaceful civil resistance, the uprising was not without violence. The streets of the Shia villages became nightly battlegrounds, with young protesters throwing stones and Molotov cocktails at the police, who responded with tear gas and birdshot. Barricades of burning tires became a common sight, blanketing the villages in an acrid black smoke. As the conflict dragged on, it escalated. A series of arson attacks and bombings targeted banks, shopping centers, and restaurants. These attacks, which killed several foreign workers, were disavowed by the mainstream opposition leaders like Sheikh al-Jamri, who blamed them on government agents seeking to discredit the movement. The government, in turn, pointed to them as proof of a foreign-backed terrorist campaign, often pointing the finger at Iran. The government's security-focused narrative was bolstered in June 1996 when it announced it had uncovered a plot by a local militant group it called "Hezbollah-Bahrain," which it claimed was an armed wing of the opposition trained and directed by Iran.

The international response was muted. The United States, whose Navy's Fifth Fleet was headquartered in Manama, and the United Kingdom, Bahrain's historic protector, found themselves in a difficult position. They publicly called for restraint on both sides but refrained from any serious pressure on the government. Stability in a key strategic ally, which hosted a vital Western military presence, took precedence over concerns about democracy and human rights.

By the late 1990s, the country was locked in a grim stalemate. The government's security crackdown had succeeded in containing the protests and preventing them from escalating into a full-blown revolution, but it had failed to extinguish the underlying causes of the unrest. The opposition had demonstrated its ability to mobilize a significant portion of the population and make the country ungovernable in certain areas, but it lacked the power to force the government to concede to its core demands. The economy was suffering, the country's international reputation was damaged, and society was deeply polarized. Bahrain seemed trapped in an endless cycle of protest and repression.

The unexpected death of the Amir, Sheikh Isa bin Salman Al Khalifa, from a heart attack on March 6, 1999, brought this era to a sudden and dramatic close. After 38 years on the throne, the ruler who had overseen Bahrain's independence and its subsequent political turmoil was gone. His reign had transformed Bahrain into a modern financial hub, but he also left behind a legacy of unresolved political conflict and a deeply divided society. He was immediately succeeded by his eldest son, the Crown Prince, Sheikh Hamad bin Isa Al Khalifa.

The change in leadership brought an immediate change in tone. The new Amir, who had been commander-in-chief of the defence force, was from a new generation and seemed to recognize that the security-first approach of his father and uncle had failed. He quickly signaled a desire for a fresh start, reaching out to the opposition and promising a new era of reform and reconciliation. The long, difficult chapter of the 1990s uprising was over. A new one, filled with cautious hope for a more open and inclusive political future, was about to begin.

CHAPTER SEVENTEEN: A New Century, A New Charter: The National Action Charter of 2001

The death of an autocrat often unleashes chaos, but the passing of Sheikh Isa bin Salman Al Khalifa on March 6, 1999, did the opposite. It broke a grim political fever that had gripped Bahrain for nearly five years. The country was exhausted by the stalemate of the 1990s uprising, a low-grade civil conflict of street protests and state repression that had left society deeply scarred and polarized. Into this tense and weary atmosphere stepped the late Amir's son, Sheikh Hamad bin Isa Al Khalifa. At forty-nine years old, the new Amir was a product of a different era. British-educated at Sandhurst and trained at the United States Army Command and General Staff College in Fort Leavenworth, Kansas, he was a military man who seemed to grasp a fundamental truth that had eluded the old guard: a purely security-based solution had failed. The country did not need a firmer hand; it needed a fresh start.

The signals came quickly, and they were unmistakable. The new Amir began his reign not with threats, but with gestures of reconciliation. He initiated a series of quiet, and then public, meetings with opposition figures, including those who had been imprisoned or exiled. He spoke a new language, one of dialogue, national unity, and a shared future. For a populace accustomed to the uncompromising rhetoric of the past, this change in tone was as startling as it was welcome. A cautious but palpable sense of hope began to ripple through the villages that had been the epicenters of the uprising.

The gestures soon turned into substantive action. In a series of dramatic moves, Sheikh Hamad began to dismantle the architecture of the security state that had been built up over the preceding quarter-century. He ordered the release of hundreds of political prisoners, many of whom had been held for years without trial. The most significant of these was the spiritual leader of the 1990s movement, Sheikh Abdulamir al-Jamri. His release from prison in July 1999, though initially to house arrest, was a hugely symbolic moment, a clear sign that the new ruler was serious about turning a page.

Simultaneously, the doors were opened for those who had been forced into exile. A general amnesty was announced, inviting the hundreds of activists, clerics, and intellectuals who had fled the country to return home without fear of prosecution. Soon, planes arriving from London, Damascus, and other centers of the Bahraini diaspora were filled with men who had not seen their families in years. Figures from the London-based Bahrain Freedom Movement, who had for years run a relentless international media campaign against the government, were welcomed back. The government even took the extraordinary step of abolishing the State Security Law, the draconian 1974 decree that had given the security services sweeping powers of arbitrary arrest and detention. The infamous State Security Court, which had operated outside the regular judicial system, was also dissolved. In the space of a few months, the pillars of the old repressive order had been pulled down.

With the political atmosphere transformed from one of confrontation to one of conciliation, the Amir unveiled his grand project for the nation's future. It was not to be a series of piecemeal reforms, but a new social contract between the ruler and the ruled, a foundational document that would chart a new political course for the 21st century. This was to be the National Action Charter. To draft it, the Amir appointed a forty-four-member Supreme National Committee, a carefully selected body designed to represent a broad cross-section of Bahraini society. It included liberals, Islamists, leftists, businessmen, academics, and, for the first time in such a high-level body, several women. Its mandate was to create a blueprint for a modern state.

Over several months in the year 2000, the committee deliberated, debated, and drafted the text. The document that emerged was a statement of principles that seemed to promise a revolutionary transformation of Bahrain's political system. It was a vision of a state built on the twin pillars of monarchy and democracy. Its headline promise was the establishment of a constitutional monarchy, where the ruling family would continue to govern, but within the framework of a constitution and the rule of law. It promised a clear separation of powers between the executive, legislative, and judicial branches of government.

The most electrifying pledge concerned the creation of a bicameral, or two-chamber, legislature. The Charter stated that this would consist of an appointed upper chamber, the Shura Council, and a democratically elected lower chamber, the Council of Representatives. Crucially, it promised that the elected chamber would be vested with full legislative powers. For those who remembered the elected parliament of 1973, this sounded like a restoration and an enhancement of the old dream. The Charter also contained extensive guarantees of human rights and public freedoms, explicitly protecting freedom of speech, the press, and religious belief, and ensuring equality among all citizens without discrimination. It was, on paper, a remarkably liberal and progressive vision for a Gulf monarchy.

The government did not simply announce the Charter; it put it to the people. A national referendum was scheduled for February 14th and 15th, 2001. This was an unprecedented move in the region, a direct appeal to the populace to endorse the new political framework. An enormous public relations campaign was launched to explain the Charter's merits and encourage a 'yes' vote. The state-controlled media was filled with optimistic coverage, and public spaces were festooned with banners celebrating the dawn of a new era.

The opposition faced a critical choice. After decades of struggle, they were being offered a path to political participation, but it was one designed and offered by the ruler. Some were skeptical, fearing a trap or a document whose lofty promises would never be implemented. However, the sheer scale of the reforms already enacted, particularly the release of prisoners and the abolition of the security law, had built a considerable reserve of goodwill. The spiritual leader Sheikh al-Jamri, after studying the document, gave it his crucial blessing, urging his followers to vote in favor. This endorsement was decisive. The main opposition groups, both religious and secular, swung their support behind the Charter, calling on Bahrainis to embrace this historic opportunity for reform.

The result of the referendum was a spectacle of national unity. The official tally was overwhelming: 98.4% of voters cast their ballots in favor of the National Action Charter, with a turnout of over 90%. The days of the vote were marked by a carnival-like atmosphere. The deep divisions of the 1990s seemed to melt away in a shared sense of optimism. It was a moment of profound national consensus, a collective embrace of a more democratic and inclusive future. The Amir, riding a wave of unprecedented popularity, hailed the result as a mandate for change and a new beginning for the nation.

In the immediate aftermath of this triumph, Sheikh Hamad took another symbolic step. On the first anniversary of the referendum, February 14, 2002, he declared that Bahrain would no longer be a "State" but a "Kingdom," and that his own title would change from Amir to King. This was presented as a modernizing move, aligning Bahrain with other constitutional monarchies around the world, such as those in the United Kingdom or Jordan. It was a change in style that was meant to reflect the change in substance promised by the Charter.

The next step was to translate the Charter's principles into law by producing a new constitution. It was here that the spirit of national unity began to fray. The opposition had assumed that the new constitution would be drafted by an elected assembly, just as the 1973 constitution had been. They argued this was the only legitimate way to create a founding charter for a new democratic era. The government, however, had other ideas. It argued that the 98.4% vote for the Charter gave the ruler the authority to implement it as he saw fit. Instead of calling for elections for a constituent assembly, the King promulgated the new constitution by royal decree in February 2002. It was a unilateral act that took the opposition completely by surprise.

When the text of the 2002 Constitution was released, the opposition's surprise turned to a deep sense of betrayal. The document did indeed establish a bicameral legislature, just as the Charter had promised. However, the details of its structure represented a radical departure from their expectations. While the 1973 constitution had established a single, powerful, elected chamber, the 2002 constitution created two chambers with equal power. The lower house, the Council of Representatives, would have forty elected members. The upper house, the Shura Council, would also have forty members, but they would be appointed directly by the King.

The critical clause was the one that stipulated that both chambers had to approve a piece of legislation for it to become law. This meant that the forty appointed members of the Shura Council could veto any bill passed by the forty elected members of the Council of Representatives. In the eyes of the opposition, this single mechanism neutered the new parliament before it had even met. It effectively halved the power of the people's elected representatives, making them partners with an unelected body of royal appointees. They had voted for a charter that promised a powerful elected legislature, but they had received a constitution that, in their view, guaranteed the executive branch ultimate control.

This schism defined the next phase of Bahrain's political life. The main opposition societies, which had coalesced into a formal political movement, with the Shia Islamist Al Wefaq National Islamic Society emerging as the largest, felt they had been deceived. They argued that the 2002 constitution was a violation of the "contract" of the National Action Charter that the people had voted for. They believed they had endorsed a return to the spirit of the 1973 constitution, only to be presented with a system that entrenched the power of the monarchy behind a democratic façade.

Their response was to boycott the parliamentary elections scheduled for October 2002. They refused to participate in a system they now considered illegitimate. The elections went ahead without them, resulting in a parliament composed largely of pro-government independents and Sunni Islamists, a body that lacked broad representation and was seen by a large segment of the population as a rubber stamp. The political honeymoon was officially over.

Despite the deep political disappointment of the opposition, the reform era did usher in significant social changes. The 2002 constitution, for the first time in Bahrain's history, granted women the right to vote and to stand for political office. While no women were successful in the boycotted 2002 elections, the King appointed six women to the forty-member Shura Council. In 2004, Dr. Nada Haffadh was appointed Minister of Health, becoming the first woman to hold a cabinet position in Bahrain. Municipal elections were also revived, allowing for a degree of local democracy.

By the middle of the decade, Bahrain had a new political reality. The climate of fear from the 1990s was gone, and there was a greater margin for political expression and organization than at any point in the country's recent history. A parliament was meeting, and elections were being held. Yet the fundamental consensus that had produced the stunning 98.4% vote for the National Action Charter had fractured. The nation was left with a contested political system, with the government insisting it had fulfilled its promises and a powerful, organized opposition insisting that the most important promise—that of a truly representative and empowered parliament—had been broken. The new century had indeed brought a new charter, but it had not brought a lasting political settlement. The unresolved questions of 2002 would continue to echo through the decade, setting the stage for a far more profound confrontation to come.

CHAPTER EIGHTEEN: Beyond the Oil Fields: Economic Diversification and Finance

There is a unique anxiety that comes with being first. For a runner, it is the pressure of holding the lead. For a nation built on a finite resource, it is the quiet, creeping knowledge that the well will one day run dry. Bahrain was the first state on the Arab side of the Gulf to discover oil, a discovery that saved it from the economic abyss of the collapsed pearl industry. But its good fortune was modest. The oil fields of Jebel Dukhan were a gentle sigh compared to the earth-shattering roars of crude that lay beneath the sands of its neighbors. This geological reality instilled a sense of pragmatism, and indeed urgency, in Bahrain's leadership that was absent elsewhere. From the very beginning of the oil era, the question was not *if* the oil would run out, but *what would come next*.

The initial answers to that question, conceived in the optimistic first decade of independence, were bold and forged in fire and steel. The Aluminium Bahrain (Alba) smelter and the Arab Shipbuilding and Repair Yard (ASRY) were titanic industrial projects, designed to give the economy a solid, non-oil foundation. The most audacious move, however, was the 1975 decision to create a hub for Offshore Banking Units (OBUs), a masterstroke of timing that captured the vast torrent of petrodollars sloshing around the region after the oil price shock. These were the foundational pillars. The task of the 1980s and 1990s was to build a skyscraper on that foundation, to transform Bahrain from a country with a few diversified industries into a truly diversified economy.

The financial sector was the designated jewel in the crown. Throughout the turmoil of the Iran-Iraq War, Manama's reputation as a safe, stable, and well-regulated haven for capital only grew. While bombs fell elsewhere, bankers in Bahrain's growing financial district were quietly and efficiently managing the wealth of the region. The Bahrain Monetary Agency (BMA), the precursor to the central bank, earned a gold-plated reputation for its rigorous but fair oversight. Unlike some of its more freewheeling global counterparts, the BMA was seen as a serious and reliable regulator, a perception that became one of the country's most valuable intangible assets. International banks that had flocked to Bahrain in the 1970s stayed and expanded their operations, cementing the island's status as the undisputed financial capital of the Middle East.

As the conventional banking sector matured, a new and potentially even more significant opportunity emerged: Islamic finance. For decades, the concept of banking that complied with Sharia law—forbidding the payment or receipt of interest (*riba*) and promoting risk-sharing principles—was a niche, almost theoretical, field. By the 1980s, it was beginning to blossom into a global industry, and Bahrain was determined to become its center of gravity. The government moved decisively to create a legal and regulatory framework that would nurture this nascent sector. It licensed the first Islamic banks, encouraged the development of Sharia-compliant financial products, and actively promoted the island as the intellectual and commercial hub for the industry.

This was not simply a matter of attracting existing Islamic banks. Bahrain sought to build the industry's very architecture. In 1991, it became the headquarters for the newly established Accounting and Auditing Organization for Islamic Financial Institutions (AAOIFI), a body created to set global standards for Islamic financial products, much like the IFRS does for conventional accounting. This was a major coup, lending immense credibility to Bahrain's claim as the industry leader. It was akin to having the world's chief referee based in your home stadium. The country became a laboratory for financial innovation, pioneering the development of *sukuk*, or Islamic bonds, which allowed governments and corporations to raise capital in a Sharia-compliant manner. By the turn of the millennium, Bahrain was not just a participant in the Islamic finance industry; it was, in many respects, its global standard-bearer.

While the bankers in their air-conditioned towers traded in complex financial instruments, the second pillar of the economy was dealing in a more tangible, and much hotter, commodity. Aluminium Bahrain, the great industrial bet of the early 1970s, was an unqualified success. Its strategic advantage was cheap energy; the smelter was effectively a way to convert the country's abundant natural gas into a solid, exportable, and high-value product. Recognizing this, the government embarked on a series of massive expansion projects. The addition of a fourth production line in 1992 and a fifth in 2005 transformed Alba from a large regional player into one of the biggest single-site aluminium smelters on the planet.

This growth had a powerful multiplier effect. The sheer volume of molten metal being produced at Alba spurred the creation of a whole ecosystem of downstream industries. A cluster of factories sprang up around the smelter, drawing on its output to manufacture a vast range of finished and semi-finished goods. Companies like Gulf Aluminium Rolling Mill (Garmco) produced high-quality rolled sheets and coils. Midal Cables became a major international supplier of aluminium rods and electrical conductors. Other factories produced everything from atomized aluminium powder to door frames and wheels. This was diversification in action, moving the country up the value chain from simply exporting a raw commodity to manufacturing and exporting sophisticated industrial products, creating thousands of skilled jobs in the process.

The third pillar of the post-oil strategy was to leverage Bahrain's unique geography and social landscape. The opening of the King Fahd Causeway in 1986 was a game-changer. What was on the surface a magnificent piece of infrastructure was, in reality, a strategic and economic umbilical cord. The causeway physically anchored Bahrain to the vast market of its giant neighbor, Saudi Arabia. Almost overnight, it transformed the tourism and retail sectors. For residents of Saudi Arabia's Eastern Province, Bahrain, with its more relaxed social environment, cinemas, and restaurants, became the go-to weekend destination. Manama's hotels filled up, its shopping malls bustled with Saudi families, and a vibrant hospitality industry flourished. The causeway turned Bahrain into the unofficial entertainment capital of the upper Gulf.

This success in regional tourism emboldened the country's leadership to think on a grander, global scale. The challenge was how to put a small island nation, known in the wider world primarily for banking and perhaps a brief mention in news reports about Gulf conflicts, onto the global map. The answer, conceived in the late 1990s under the enthusiastic patronage of the new Amir, Sheikh Hamad, was a spectacle of speed, noise, and glamour: Formula 1. The decision to build a state-of-the-art racetrack in the middle of the Sakhir desert was an audacious gamble, costing hundreds of millions of dollars. To many observers, it seemed a spectacular folly.

The Bahrain International Circuit opened in 2004, hosting the first-ever Formula 1 Grand Prix in the Middle East. The event was a triumph of marketing and logistics. The image of high-tech racing cars screaming through the desert, framed by palm trees and futuristic architecture, was broadcast to hundreds of millions of people around the world. It was a powerful statement. It announced that Bahrain was modern, open for business, and capable of hosting world-class events. The Grand Prix was never about making a direct profit from ticket sales; it was a multi-million-dollar advertisement for "Brand Bahrain." It was designed to attract investment, boost the tourism and hospitality sectors, and reframe the international perception of the country.

Underpinning all these efforts was a conscious policy of investing in people. Bahrain's leaders understood that a diversified, knowledge-based economy could not be run on imported labor alone. The early investments in public education had created one of the most literate and skilled populations in the region. The challenge was to match those skills with the demands of the new economy. This led to the policy of "Bahrainization," a concerted effort to increase the percentage of Bahraini nationals employed in the private sector. The government established training institutes, most notably the Bahrain Training Institute (BTI), and introduced levy systems that incentivized companies to hire and train local talent.

This process was overseen by new, dynamic government bodies designed to cut through bureaucracy and drive the reform agenda. The most important of these was the Economic Development Board (EDB), established in 2000. Chaired by the Crown Prince, Sheikh Salman bin Hamad Al Khalifa, the EDB was staffed by a mix of high-ranking officials and private sector leaders and acted as a powerful super-agency, tasked with attracting foreign investment and steering the overall economic strategy.

The first decade of the 21st century was the high-water mark of this economic model. High oil prices provided the government with a massive financial cushion, allowing it to invest heavily in infrastructure and signature projects. Manama's skyline was transformed by a forest of cranes. The Bahrain Financial Harbour and the Bahrain World Trade Center, with its iconic integrated wind turbines, rose from reclaimed land, gleaming new temples to the country's financial ambitions. The economy was booming, growing at a healthy clip, and the country seemed to have successfully navigated the transition to a post-oil future. This confidence was formally codified in October 2008 with the launch of "Economic Vision 2030," a comprehensive national strategy designed to guide the next phase of development.

Just as this ambitious vision was being unveiled, however, the world's financial system was imploding. The global financial crisis that began in 2008 sent a shockwave through the international banking sector. For Bahrain, a country that had staked so much of its future on becoming a financial hub, it was the first great stress test of its diversified model. The crisis hit the investment banks and real estate projects particularly hard, forcing a painful period of consolidation and deleveraging. Yet, the system, overseen by a newly empowered Central Bank of Bahrain (which had replaced the BMA in 2006), proved surprisingly resilient. There were no catastrophic bank failures, and the core of the financial system held firm. The country had built an economy that could bend without breaking. It had successfully moved beyond the oil fields, but the new landscape it had created would soon be shaken by a very different kind of crisis, one that originated not in the boardrooms of New York, but in its own towns and villages.

CHAPTER NINETEEN: The Tumult of 2011: The Pearl Roundabout Protests

For a decade, the political settlement promised by the National Action Charter had held, but it had not healed. The grand consensus of 2001 had fractured into a familiar landscape of government intransigence and opposition frustration. The cycle of parliamentary boycotts and pro-government majorities, of street protests and security crackdowns, had become the country's grinding new normal. Then, in the first weeks of 2011, the entire Arab world seemed to catch fire. From the shores of Tunisia, the self-immolation of a street vendor named Mohamed Bouazizi had ignited a revolutionary wildfire that was sweeping away decades of autocratic rule. First, Tunisia's Zine El Abidine Ben Ali was gone. Then, on February 11th, after eighteen days of colossal protests in Cairo's Tahrir Square, Egypt's Hosni Mubarak fell. The impossible was suddenly happening, and for a new generation of activists connected by Facebook and Twitter, the lesson was electrifying: change did not have to come through slow, frustrating negotiations; it could be seized on the streets.

In Bahrain, this new sense of possibility found a natural focus. Anonymous online activists, inspired by the events in Tunis and Cairo, put out a call for a "Day of Rage." The date they chose was deeply symbolic: February 14th, the tenth anniversary of the referendum on the National Action Charter. It was a date that encapsulated the entire arc of hope and disappointment, a direct appeal to the memory of a promise the opposition felt had been profoundly broken. The demands were a familiar echo of the past two decades: an end to corruption and sectarian discrimination, the release of political prisoners, a new constitution, and a genuinely representative government. The government, wary of the regional mood, tried to pre-empt the protests with a series of popular concessions, offering cash handouts to families and promising greater media freedom. But the momentum was unstoppable.

On Monday, February 14th, the protests began. They were not concentrated in the capital but scattered across the country's predominantly Shia villages. In the village of Al Daih, a small crowd gathered. Security forces moved in to disperse them, and in the ensuing confrontation, a 21-year-old protester named Ali Abdulhadi Mushaima was shot in the back with birdshot at close range. He died from his injuries. The first day of protest had produced its first martyr. The next day, as a vast and emotional crowd carried Mushaima's body to be buried, the cycle repeated itself. Clashes broke out between mourners and riot police near the cemetery in Jidhafs. Another protester, 31-year-old Fadhel Al-Matrook, was killed, again by shotgun pellets fired at close range.

The two deaths in two days transformed the political atmosphere from tense to explosive. The main opposition political society, Al Wefaq, which had been hesitant to fully endorse the street protests, now suspended its participation in parliament in protest. That evening, something snapped. As news of the second death spread, the police, who had been clashing with mourners, suddenly pulled back from the streets of the capital. It was a tactical withdrawal, but it created a power vacuum. Sensing the opportunity, thousands of protesters who had been marching from the funeral procession began to stream towards the heart of Manama. Their destination was a large, grassy traffic circle dominated by a soaring white monument of six dhow sails holding a single pearl aloft. Officially named the GCC Roundabout, to the world it would soon become known simply as the Pearl Roundabout. It was about to become the epicenter of the Bahraini uprising.

By nightfall on February 15th, the roundabout was occupied. Emulating the protesters in Tahrir Square, the demonstrators set up a tent city. Food stalls, medical clinics, and media centers sprang up. A stage was erected, and a stream of speakers—activists, clerics, poets, and ordinary citizens—addressed the growing crowds. The atmosphere was a heady mix of festival and revolution. It was a space unlike any that had existed in Bahrain before, a zone of free expression where the normal rules of fear and deference were suspended. Sunnis and Shias mingled, families brought their children, and political debates raged late into the night. Banners called for the fall of the Prime Minister, Sheikh Khalifa bin Salman, who had been in office since before independence and was seen as the primary obstacle to reform. For a few days, the Pearl Roundabout was the liberated capital of a new Bahrain.

The government, after its initial withdrawal, was watching with mounting alarm. From its perspective, the occupation of a key intersection in the heart of the financial district was not a peaceful protest but an illegal and dangerous seizure of public space that was paralyzing the country. In the early hours of Thursday, February 17th, it decided to act. Just after 3:00 a.m., while the vast majority of the thousands of protesters were asleep in their tents, the security forces attacked. Hundreds of riot police, backed by armored vehicles, moved in from all sides without warning. They fired massive volleys of tear gas into the encampment and advanced with shotguns, sound grenades, and clubs. The scene was one of utter chaos and terror. People were woken from their sleep by the sound of explosions and the suffocating clouds of gas, trampled in the stampede as they tried to flee. Four people were killed in the raid and hundreds were injured, many with horrific wounds from birdshot fired at point-blank range. By dawn, the roundabout was clear, its grass stained with blood and littered with the abandoned debris of the encampment. The day would be forever known to the opposition as "Bloody Thursday."

The raid was a catastrophic miscalculation. It was intended to crush the movement with a single, decisive blow, but instead, it galvanized it. The sheer brutality of the attack, launched against sleeping protesters, horrified the nation and drew widespread international condemnation. The Al Wefaq bloc, which had only suspended its participation in parliament, now resigned entirely. The General Federation of Bahrain Trade Unions called for a general strike. The country was on the verge of a complete shutdown. In the aftermath of the raid, the military was deployed onto the streets, with tanks and armored personnel carriers taking up positions at key intersections, enforcing a de facto state of martial law.

The crisis had reached a tipping point, and into this volatile situation stepped the Crown Prince, Sheikh Salman bin Hamad Al Khalifa. Seen as the leading modernizer and reformer within the royal family, he appeared on state television to offer a path back from the brink. In a somber address, he offered his condolences for the lives lost and called for calm. Crucially, he promised to lead a national dialogue to address the protesters' grievances once the military had withdrawn and life had returned to normal. To show his sincerity, on February 18th, he ordered the army tanks and troops to pull back from the streets and from the Pearl Roundabout.

The military withdrawal was another pivotal moment. On Saturday, February 19th, the protesters, who had been gathering in their thousands at the Salmaniya hospital complex where the injured were being treated, began to march. They headed back towards the empty roundabout. This time, there was no one to stop them. Cheering and waving national flags, they flooded back into the circle, re-establishing their camp, this time in far greater numbers and with a hardened sense of resolve. The re-occupation was a stunning victory for the protest movement. What followed was the high-water mark of the uprising. On February 22nd, a vast procession, estimated by some at over 100,000 people—a significant fraction of the country's citizen population—marched through the streets of Manama in what was dubbed the "March of Loyalty to the Martyrs."

The sheer scale of the movement had shifted the political ground. The Crown Prince's initiative for dialogue began, but the two sides were moving further apart. The protest movement was now a loose coalition of seven opposition groups, with the Shia Islamist Al Wefaq being the largest and most organized. Their initial demands for reform were now accompanied by a set of non-negotiable preconditions for dialogue, including the resignation of the government and an investigation into the killings. But within the roundabout, a more radical current was gaining strength. For a growing number of protesters, particularly the younger generation of activists who had initiated the "Day of Rage," the goal was no longer the reform of the system, but its complete overthrow. The slogan "Down, down Hamad" began to be heard, a direct challenge to the King himself.

This radicalization, in turn, fueled a powerful counter-reaction. The spectacle of a major intersection being occupied by an overwhelmingly Shia-led protest movement, with some banners featuring the images of Iranian and Lebanese Shia clerics, stoked deep anxieties within the country's Sunni community. They feared a sectarian takeover, an "Islamic revolution" that would upend the country's traditional power structure and align it with Iran. Pro-government rallies began to be held, with thousands of Sunnis gathering to wave pictures of the King and the Prime Minister, pledging their loyalty to the monarchy. The state media amplified this narrative, increasingly framing the protest movement not as a legitimate call for democratic reform, but as a dangerous, sectarian, and foreign-backed plot. The national unity that had been a hallmark of the first days in the roundabout was fracturing along a sharp sectarian fault line.

The Crown Prince's dialogue initiative faltered in this atmosphere of mutual suspicion and escalating demands. By early March, the country was effectively paralyzed. Protesters from the roundabout began a series of high-profile marches, attempting to blockade the Financial Harbour, the symbol of Bahrain's modern economy. Another group marched on the Royal Court in Riffa, the heart of the Al Khalifa's traditional power base. Clashes between protesters and pro-government civilians became more frequent and violent. The state was losing control of the streets, and the economy was grinding to a halt. For the government and its allies in the Gulf, the situation was becoming untenable.

The decision was made to seek outside help. On Monday, March 14th, a convoy of armored vehicles flying the flag of Saudi Arabia rolled across the King Fahd Causeway and into Bahrain. They were soon joined by a contingent of police from the United Arab Emirates. This was the Peninsula Shield Force, the joint military arm of the Gulf Cooperation Council, responding to a formal request from the government of Bahrain. The official rationale was that the forces were being deployed to protect Bahrain's key strategic infrastructure—power plants, oil refineries, and financial centers—thus freeing up Bahrain's own security forces to deal with the street protests and restore order.

For the opposition and its supporters, this was nothing less than a foreign invasion. They saw the arrival of Saudi tanks as a declaration of war on a domestic protest movement, a clear sign that the regime had abandoned any pretense of dialogue and had opted for a military solution. The arrival of the GCC forces was the point of no return. The next day, March 15th, King Hamad declared a three-month State of National Safety, effectively imposing martial law.

The crackdown that followed was swift, methodical, and overwhelming. In the early morning of March 16th, a massive force of Bahraini police and soldiers, backed by armored vehicles and helicopters, moved to clear the Pearl Roundabout for the final time. This was not a repeat of the chaotic raid of a month earlier. It was a full-scale military-style operation. They advanced behind a wall of tear gas, systematically clearing the area and pushing the remaining protesters out into the surrounding neighborhoods. Several more protesters were killed in the operation. By midday, the roundabout, which for one month had been the symbol of a revolution, was an empty, smoldering patch of ground under military occupation.

The crackdown did not stop at the roundabout. It fanned out into the Shia villages, which were placed under a tight military cordon. House-to-house raids began, and a wave of mass arrests swept up thousands of people—not just protesters, but doctors and nurses who had treated the injured, teachers, athletes, and human rights activists. The state was determined not only to end the protest but to dismantle the entire network of people it believed had supported it. Two days later, on the morning of March 18th, army cranes and bulldozers moved into the now-empty Pearl Roundabout. In a final, symbolic act of erasure, they began to tear down the iconic monument, piece by piece, until nothing was left. The physical heart of the uprising had been surgically removed from the city.

The state wanted to ensure that no trace of the month of tumult remained.

CHAPTER TWENTY: A Decade of Reckoning: The Aftermath of the Uprising

The demolition of the Pearl Monument was not an end, but a beginning. It was the first act in a methodical and sweeping campaign to erase the uprising not just from the city's landscape, but from its political life. With the arrival of the Peninsula Shield Force and the declaration of a three-month State of National Safety on March 15, 2011, the government's approach shifted from containment to retribution. The brief, heady days of the tent city gave way to a grim and protracted decade of reckoning. The state, having stared into what it considered the abyss of a sectarian, foreign-backed revolution, was now determined to re-establish its authority, utterly and completely.

The initial phase was a security operation of overwhelming force. The Shia villages that had been the heartlands of the protest were placed under a tight military cordon, with checkpoints manned by soldiers and masked police creating an atmosphere of collective punishment. Night raids became a terrifyingly common occurrence. Security forces would descend on homes in the pre-dawn hours, smashing down doors and dragging away suspected activists. The official justification was the pursuit of criminals and saboteurs, but the net was cast far wider. Thousands were arrested in the weeks and months that followed: students, teachers, bloggers, athletes, and, most controversially, dozens of doctors, nurses, and paramedics from the Salmaniya Medical Complex, the main public hospital. Their crime, in the eyes of the state, was having provided medical treatment to injured protesters, an act that was reframed as collaboration with the opposition.

A parallel purge was conducted across the public and private sectors. State-owned enterprises, from the national airline Gulf Air to the industrial giant Aluminium Bahrain, launched disciplinary proceedings against hundreds of employees who had participated in the general strike called by the trade unions. Loyalty was the new watchword, and anyone suspected of sympathizing with the protest movement was at risk. University students who had demonstrated were expelled, their scholarships revoked. Even the country's national football team was not immune, with several prominent Shia players being dismissed and publicly shamed on state television for their alleged participation in protests. The message was unambiguous: there would be a steep price for dissent.

To process the thousands of detainees, the government established special military tribunals called the National Safety Courts. These courts operated under martial law, with military judges presiding over swift trials that lacked the most basic standards of due process. Defendants often had limited access to lawyers, were not allowed to present a proper defense, and were convicted on the basis of confessions that many claimed were extracted under torture. In these courts, twenty-one of the most prominent political leaders and human rights activists, who came to be known as the "Bahrain 13," were sentenced to long prison terms, including life imprisonment for figures like Abdulhadi al-Khawaja and Abdulwahab Hussain. Two men were sentenced to death and executed for the killing of a police officer, following trials that were condemned internationally as grossly unfair.

The sheer ferocity of the crackdown, particularly the reports of widespread torture and deaths in custody, drew a storm of international condemnation. Bahrain, which had spent a decade carefully cultivating an image as a modern, reforming monarchy and a stable financial hub, now found itself a pariah in the eyes of human rights organizations. The government, sensitive to the damage being done to its international reputation and under pressure from key allies like the United States and the United Kingdom, recognized that a purely security-based response was unsustainable. It needed a way to address the international criticism without conceding the legitimacy of the uprising itself.

The solution was an act of extraordinary political theatre. In June 2011, King Hamad announced the establishment of the Bahrain Independent Commission of Inquiry (BICI). This was not to be an internal government committee. The King invited a panel of internationally renowned legal experts, headed by the distinguished Egyptian-American jurist Professor M. Cherif Bassiouni, to conduct a fully independent investigation into the events of February and March and their aftermath. The commission was given a broad mandate, unfettered access, and the power to make its findings and recommendations public. It was a high-stakes gamble, an unprecedented move for any state in the region that had just crushed a major popular uprising.

For five months, Bassiouni and his team worked meticulously. They established an office in Manama, reviewed over nine thousand official documents, and took testimony from thousands of individuals, from government ministers and security chiefs to victims of abuse and the families of those killed. The atmosphere in the country was thick with fear, but the BICI became a space where people felt they could tell their stories. In November 2011, the commission delivered its 500-page report. It was presented to the King in a televised ceremony, a moment of riveting political drama.

The BICI report was a bombshell. While it absolved the government of a systematic policy of killing protesters, it was a thorough and damning indictment of the state's conduct. It methodically documented 35 deaths, including five security personnel and five individuals who died as a result of torture in custody. It confirmed the "systematic" use of torture and physical and psychological coercion against detainees. It found that the security forces had used excessive and unnecessary force against protesters. It detailed the unfair trials in the National Safety Courts and the mass dismissal of workers and students as a form of collective punishment. Crucially, the commission stated that it had found no discernible evidence of Iranian involvement in the uprising, directly contradicting the government's core narrative. The report concluded with a set of 26 detailed recommendations, calling for the creation of independent oversight bodies for the security services, a full investigation into all allegations of torture, the reinstatement of sacked workers, and the release of those imprisoned for exercising their right to free speech.

In a move that stunned many observers, King Hamad publicly accepted the report's findings and pledged to implement its recommendations. It was a moment of profound possibility, a potential turning point that could have paved the way for genuine reconciliation. The government moved with some speed on the institutional reforms. The notorious National Security Agency was stripped of its powers of arrest. An independent Ombudsman's office within the Ministry of Interior and a Special Investigation Unit within the Public Prosecution were created to handle complaints against the police. A compensation fund was established for victims and their families.

However, for the opposition and for international human rights groups, the implementation fell far short of the report's spirit. While some low-ranking police officers were prosecuted for abuse, no senior officials were ever held accountable for the systematic torture and killings documented by the BICI. The opposition argued that the new oversight bodies lacked genuine independence and power, serving more as a public relations exercise than a mechanism for real accountability. The core political grievances that had fueled the uprising—the demand for a representative government, an end to sectarian discrimination, and a new constitution—were not even part of the BICI's mandate. The report had masterfully documented the symptoms, but it had not been allowed to prescribe a cure for the underlying disease.

While the government engaged with the BICI process, the situation on the ground remained volatile. The security crackdown had ended the mass demonstrations in the capital, but it had not pacified the country. The conflict retreated into the Shia villages, where it became a nightly, grinding war of attrition. Young protesters, now more radicalized than ever, clashed with riot police, throwing Molotov cocktails and blocking roads with burning tires. The police responded with relentless raids and what became known as "collective punishment by tear gas," firing huge volumes of the chemical agent into residential areas, often directly into homes. Funerals for those who died in the ongoing clashes, or from the effects of tear gas, became the new flashpoints for major confrontations.

In an attempt to find a political solution, the government launched a National Dialogue in July 2011. However, with the main opposition leaders in prison and the largest political society, Al Wefaq, boycotting the process due to the ongoing crackdown, the dialogue was widely seen as illegitimate. It was dominated by pro-government figures and failed to produce any meaningful political reforms. Subsequent attempts at dialogue in 2013 and 2014, even with Al Wefaq's participation, also collapsed amidst mutual recrimination. The government offered only minor concessions, while the opposition continued to demand fundamental changes to the structure of power, including an elected prime minister and a parliament with full legislative authority. The gap was unbridgeable.

Frustrated by the political stalemate and the continued repression, the opposition's street-level tactics became more confrontational. A new and more militant youth coalition, the February 14 Youth Coalition, emerged, organizing protests and openly calling for the downfall of the monarchy. There was also an increase in violence, with a number of sophisticated bomb attacks targeting police patrols, killing several officers. The government seized on these attacks as proof that the opposition was a terrorist movement, a narrative it used to justify a final, decisive move to eliminate all organized political dissent.

The reckoning now turned on the legal opposition societies themselves. The state, having failed to co-opt them through dialogue, decided to dismantle them. In 2012, the citizenship of 31 prominent activists was revoked by administrative order. This tactic of rendering critics stateless would be expanded dramatically in the following years, affecting hundreds of individuals. Then the focus turned to the leadership. In 2014, after giving a speech critical of the government, Sheikh Ali Salman, the leader of Al Wefaq, was arrested. He was subsequently sentenced to four years in prison for inciting disobedience, a sentence that was later increased to life imprisonment on new charges of spying for Qatar. The imprisonment of the country's most prominent mainstream opposition leader sent a chilling message.

The final act came in 2016. A Bahraini court ordered the dissolution of Al Wefaq, seizing its assets and banning its activities. The government accused the society of creating an environment for terrorism and extremism. A year later, in May 2017, the same fate befell the country's main secular opposition group, the National Democratic Action Society, or Wa'ad. With the main religious and secular opposition parties banned and their leaders in prison or in exile, the last vestiges of organized, legal political opposition had been extinguished. To complete the process, a new law was passed in 2016 banning former members of dissolved political societies from running for parliament, effectively locking the entire opposition out of the political process for good.

The economic cost of this decade of turmoil was significant. The 2011 Formula 1 Grand Prix, the country's premier international event, had to be cancelled, a major blow to both the economy and the country's image. Investor confidence was shaken, and the crucial tourism sector suffered badly. While the financial sector proved resilient, the government's spending on security and social subsidies skyrocketed as it sought to placate parts of the population with state largesse. Government debt ballooned. The country's stability was underwritten by its wealthy Gulf neighbors. In 2011, the GCC announced a ten-year, $10 billion aid package for Bahrain and Oman to fund development and blunt the appeal of the protests. In 2018, with Bahrain facing a serious credit crunch, Saudi Arabia, the UAE, and Kuwait stepped in again with another $10 billion financial support package, a clear signal that they would not allow the kingdom's economy to fail.

By the end of the decade, a new and stark reality had settled over Bahrain. The uprising had been comprehensively defeated. The state had reasserted its total control. The streets were quiet, not because the grievances had been resolved, but because the space for dissent had been almost entirely closed. The opposition was either in prison, in exile, stateless, or silenced. The political settlement of the National Action Charter, once hailed as a new dawn, was a distant memory. A deep and bitter sectarian chasm now ran through the society. The government had secured its own survival, but at the cost of the national unity it had once promised. The reckoning had been a brutal one, and its consequences would continue to shape the life of the nation for years to come.

CHAPTER TWENTY-ONE: Bahrain on the World Stage: Foreign Policy in the 21st Century

To be a small state in the Persian Gulf is to live with the constant awareness that your fate can be decided by the whims of giants. For Bahrain, an archipelago whose very existence has been shaped by the ambitions of distant empires, the 21st century has been a masterclass in the art of strategic survival. Its foreign policy is not a matter of choice, but of necessity; a complex and constantly shifting calculus designed to secure its sovereignty, protect its economy, and navigate the treacherous currents of a region in perpetual turmoil. This has required a delicate balancing act: anchoring its security in powerful patrons, binding itself to its closest neighbor, confronting its primary adversary, and, when the moment came, making bold new alliances that would have been unthinkable just a few years earlier.

The bedrock of this entire strategy, the immovable anchor to which Bahrain's foreign policy is moored, is its relationship with the Kingdom of Saudi Arabia. It is a bond that transcends a typical alliance. Forged in shared history, dynastic ties, a common monarchical system, and a near-identical worldview on regional threats, the relationship is one of profound strategic depth. Saudi Arabia is Bahrain's largest trading partner, a vital source of financial support, and, as the world saw in 2011, its ultimate security guarantor. The King Fahd Causeway is not just an economic lifeline but an umbilical cord, a physical manifestation of the promise that Bahrain will never be left to stand alone. This alignment is near-total; on almost every major regional issue, from the war in Yemen to the posture towards Iran, Manama's position is a mirror of Riyadh's. This has sometimes been characterized as a client-patron relationship, and while there is an undeniable asymmetry of power, it is viewed from Manama as a pragmatic and essential partnership for survival.

While Saudi Arabia provides the regional anchor, the ultimate security umbrella has been held by the West, primarily the United States and the United Kingdom. The relationship with Washington is institutionalized in a few square kilometers of waterfront property in the Juffair district of Manama: the headquarters of the United States Navy's Fifth Fleet. Hosting this critical instrument of American power has been the cornerstone of Bahrain's defense strategy since independence. It makes the island indispensable to American strategic interests in the Middle East, particularly the protection of vital shipping lanes and the containment of Iran. This status as a "Major Non-NATO Ally," granted in 2002, provides access to American military technology and a powerful deterrent against aggression.

The relationship was severely tested by the events of 2011. The Obama administration found itself in an agonizing position, caught between its rhetoric supporting the aspirations of the Arab Spring and its strategic imperative to maintain a stable partnership with a key military host. Washington publicly expressed its concern over the violence, gently urging dialogue and reform, and for a time, placed a hold on some arms sales to Bahrain. However, strategic interests ultimately prevailed. The core of the security relationship remained untouched, a clear signal that the Fifth Fleet's presence and the stability of the kingdom were Washington's overriding priorities.

This American security presence was complemented by the return of its historical predecessor. In a clear sign of a renewed British commitment to the region after its 1971 withdrawal, the United Kingdom announced in 2014 that it would re-establish a permanent naval base in Bahrain. The new UK Naval Support Facility, officially opened in April 2018 on the site of the old HMS Juffair, became Britain's first permanent military base east of Suez in over four decades. For Bahrain, it was a welcome deepening of a historic relationship, adding another layer to its security architecture and reinforcing its role as the key naval hub for Western powers in the Gulf.

If the alliances with Saudi Arabia and the West are the pillars of Bahrain's foreign policy, the shadow that looms over them is cast by the Islamic Republic of Iran. Since the 1979 revolution, and particularly following the discovery of an alleged Iran-sponsored coup plot in 1981, Manama has viewed Tehran as the primary existential threat to its security. This perception hardened into certainty in the 21st century. The Bahraini government consistently accused Iran of fomenting unrest among its Shia population, providing training and arms to militant cells, and waging a relentless propaganda campaign to destabilize the monarchy. Every discovery of a weapons cache or a bomb plot was, in Manama's narrative, another piece of evidence of Iran's malign intentions.

This deep-seated suspicion shaped Bahrain's reaction to international diplomacy with Tehran. When world powers negotiated the Joint Comprehensive Plan of Action (JCPOA), the 2015 nuclear deal with Iran, Bahrain was publicly skeptical. Along with Saudi Arabia and the UAE, Manama feared the deal was dangerously narrow. Bahraini officials argued that by focusing solely on the nuclear program, the agreement ignored Iran's ballistic missile development and its support for proxy militias across the region—the very activities that posed the most direct threat to Gulf security. The deal, a senior Bahraini official later lamented, "fueled crises across the Middle East" and failed to moderate Iranian behavior. Consequently, Bahrain strongly welcomed the Trump administration's decision to withdraw the United States from the JCPOA in 2018, viewing it as a vindication of its long-held concerns.

This regional cold war with Iran also drove Bahrain's policy within its own neighborhood, most dramatically during the Qatar diplomatic crisis. On June 5, 2017, Bahrain was the first country to announce it was severing all diplomatic and economic ties with Qatar, joining Saudi Arabia, the UAE, and Egypt in a full-scale blockade. The quartet accused Qatar of supporting terrorism and, most damningly, of being too close to Iran. For Bahrain, Qatar's maverick foreign policy, particularly the often critical coverage of Bahrain's internal affairs by the Al Jazeera network, was a long-standing irritant. The blockade was an opportunity to force a change in Doha's behavior and bring it firmly back into the Saudi-led fold. Bahrain adopted one of the hardest lines during the three-and-a-half-year standoff, which only formally ended with the Al-Ula Declaration in January 2021. Diplomatic ties between Manama and Doha were the last to be restored, in April 2023, illustrating the depth of the rift.

The unwavering focus on the Iranian threat was also the primary catalyst for the most dramatic foreign policy shift in Bahrain's recent history. On September 11, 2020, it was announced that Bahrain would join the United Arab Emirates in normalizing relations with the state of Israel. The agreement, part of the American-brokered "Abraham Accords," was formally signed at the White House on September 15. For decades, such a move would have been political heresy, a violation of the long-standing Arab consensus that normalization could only come after the creation of a Palestinian state. But by 2020, the strategic calculus had changed entirely.

The shared animosity towards Iran had fostered years of quiet, behind-the-scenes security and intelligence cooperation between Israel and some Gulf states. The Abraham Accords brought this de facto alliance out into the open. For Bahrain, the strategic logic was compelling. Normalization created a formal anti-Iran axis, aligning it with the region's foremost military and technological power. It was also a move that strongly aligned Manama with the foreign policy priorities of the Trump administration, its key security partner. While the official statements stressed that the deal would advance the cause of peace, and King Hamad reiterated the need for a two-state solution, the immediate driver was realpolitik. The accord opened the door for cooperation in fields from technology and tourism to intelligence sharing, formalizing a relationship built on the old principle that the enemy of my enemy is my friend.

While the kingdom's gaze remained fixed on its immediate neighborhood and its Western partners, it also began to look further east. Like its Gulf neighbors, Bahrain recognized the growing economic and geopolitical importance of China. Diplomatic relations, established in 1989, deepened significantly in the new millennium. This relationship was, and remains, overwhelmingly economic. China became Bahrain's largest source of imports, and Manama eagerly signed on to Beijing's Belt and Road Initiative, hoping to attract Chinese investment into its infrastructure and high-tech sectors. In May 2024, during a visit by King Hamad to Beijing, the two countries elevated their relationship to a "comprehensive strategic partnership." This engagement with Beijing does not represent a pivot away from the West, but rather a pragmatic diversification of its economic partnerships, a recognition of a shifting global order in which a small nation must maintain friendly relations with as many powers as possible.

CHAPTER TWENTY-TWO: The Evolution of Bahraini Society: Culture, Identity, and Modernization

To understand the soul of modern Bahraini society is to peel back the layers of a palimpsest. At its base lies the ancient, salt-sprayed identity of an island people, their fortunes tied to the rhythms of the sea. Upon this is written the story of pearling, a trade that forged a unique social hierarchy and a cosmopolitan outlook. Then, in thick, bold strokes, came the age of oil, a deluge of wealth and modernity that transformed the physical and social landscape with breathtaking speed. Finally, the turbulent events of the late 20th and early 21st centuries etched deep and often painful lines, redrawing the boundaries of community and identity. The result is a society of fascinating complexity, a place where tradition and hyper-modernity coexist, where profound social cohesion sits alongside deep sectarian division, and where a deeply rooted local culture is constantly negotiating with the powerful currents of globalization.

Before 1932, life was governed by two great forces: the date palm and the pearl. Society was settled in villages clustered around the northern coast, where freshwater springs supported lush groves of dates, the primary agricultural staple. In the towns of Manama and Muharraq, life was organized around the pearling industry. This was a society with a rigid, almost feudal, structure. At the apex were the powerful *tawashin*, the wealthy pearl merchants who financed the expeditions and controlled the trade. Below them were the *nakhudas*, the captains who commanded the dhows, and beneath them, the great mass of divers (*ghais*) and crew, many of whom were trapped in a lifelong cycle of debt. Daily life was communal and centered on the *fareej*, the neighborhood, and the mosque. It was a world of coral-stone houses with wind towers, and simple palm-frond huts known as *barastis* in the villages. This pre-oil society was already remarkably diverse, a mosaic of the indigenous *Baharna* (Shia Arabs, likely descended from the island's pre-Islamic inhabitants), Sunni Arab tribes who had migrated from the mainland (including the ruling Al Khalifa), and a significant community of Persian merchants, known as the *Ajam*. There were also long-standing communities of Indians, Balochis, and Afro-Arabs, making the pearling ports some of the most cosmopolitan centers in the Gulf.

The discovery of oil and the subsequent collapse of the pearl trade did not just change the economy; it dynamited the foundations of this old social order. The power of the great merchant families waned, and the divers, freed from their debts but stripped of their livelihood, became the first generation of industrial wage-earners. Oil revenue funded the creation of a paternalistic welfare state that provided free education, healthcare, and subsidized housing, fundamentally altering the relationship between the citizen and the state. The landscape itself was rewritten. The old towns of Manama and Muharraq expanded rapidly, and entirely new, meticulously planned towns like Isa Town and later Hamad Town sprang up from the desert, complete with modern villas, schools, and shopping centers. These new urban spaces, connected by a growing network of highways, broke down the old, insular geography of the *fareej* and created a more mobile and integrated, yet also more anonymous, society.

The most profound social change was demographic. The oil boom, and the later booms in finance and construction, required a labor force far larger than the small local population could provide. This triggered a massive influx of expatriate workers, a trend that accelerated with each decade. Today, non-nationals make up more than half of the country's total population, and an even larger majority of the workforce. This vast expatriate community is itself highly stratified. At one end are Western and Arab professionals in the finance and oil sectors, often living in comfortable residential compounds. The great majority, however, are low-wage laborers from South and Southeast Asia, who work in construction, sanitation, and domestic service. This demographic reality has made Bahrain a deeply multicultural society, a place where dozens of languages can be heard in the souqs and shopping malls. It has also created a host of complex social challenges, from the downward pressure on wages for low-skilled Bahraini workers to the social segregation that often exists between the different communities.

Central to Bahraini identity is the concept of family. The extended family remains the primary unit of social life, a source of identity, support, and obligation that often comes before all other relationships. Multi-generational households, while less common than in the past, still exist, and major life events are community affairs. Hospitality is a cherished and defining cultural value, expressed through the ritual of offering coffee and the frequent hosting of large meals for friends and family. However, the forces of modernization have placed this traditional structure under new pressures. The shift to a wage-based economy, the rise of the nuclear family living in modern apartments, and the influence of global media have all altered family dynamics and social customs.

The political turmoil of the late 20th and early 21st centuries, particularly the events of 2011, had a deeply corrosive effect on the fabric of society, hardening the lines of sectarian identity. While Sunni and Shia communities had coexisted for centuries, often in the same neighborhoods, the political conflict overlaid historical religious differences with a modern narrative of political grievance and existential threat. On one side, a narrative of marginalization and systemic discrimination took hold within the Shia community. On the other, a narrative of a loyalist Sunni community defending the state from a sectarian, foreign-backed threat was promoted. This polarization damaged the social trust that had once been a hallmark of Bahraini life. Inter-communal friendships became strained, and the number of mixed marriages, once common enough to earn the nickname "sushi" (Sunni-Shia), reportedly declined. While many Bahrainis on both sides reject this sectarian lens, the political conflict made the religious divide the most salient and painful feature of modern social identity.

In the midst of this rapid and often jarring modernization, a powerful movement to preserve and celebrate the nation's unique culture and heritage has taken root. The state, through bodies like the Bahrain Authority for Culture and Antiquities, has poured significant resources into protecting its past. The most ambitious of these projects is the Pearling Path in Muharraq, a UNESCO World Heritage Site. This meticulously restored 3.5-kilometer trail links the former homes of merchants, the *majlis* where deals were struck, and the seafront fort from which the dhows departed, creating a living museum of the era that defined the island's identity for centuries. Ancient archaeological sites, from the thousands of Dilmun-era burial mounds to the formidable Bahrain Fort, another World Heritage Site, are carefully maintained as tangible links to a history stretching back millennia.

Traditional crafts, which once faced extinction, are being actively revived. In villages like A'ali, potters still use traditional methods to shape clay from the Riffa plains, their techniques passed down through generations. In Bani Jamra and Jasra, weavers work on wooden looms, producing textiles for traditional garments, a craft now supported by cultural centers that showcase their work to tourists and new generations of Bahrainis. Basket weaving, using leaves from the abundant palm trees, continues to be a widely practiced craft, producing everything from dining mats to decorative baskets.

The nation's artistic life reflects the same blend of tradition and modernity. The rich folk music culture is still very much alive. The most distinctive of these is *sawt* ("voice"), a complex and soulful urban genre that emerged in the late 19th and early 20th centuries. Performed with the oud and a small hand-drum called the *mirwas*, sawt is a sophisticated art form that combines classical Arabic poetry with influences from across the region, and its most famous historical performers, like Mohamed Bin Fares, are national icons. Another vital musical tradition is *fidjeri*, the haunting and rhythmic call-and-response chants of the pearl divers, performed by male-only ensembles to recount the stories of the sea. Alongside this, a vibrant contemporary art scene has flourished since the mid-20th century. The Bahrain Arts Society, founded in 1983, has nurtured generations of painters and sculptors, whose work often explores themes of identity, heritage, and the rapid pace of social change.

Bahraini cuisine is, perhaps, the most accessible expression of the island's multicultural history. The national dish, *machboos*, a richly spiced rice dish served with meat or fish, is a staple of every household. The island's geography is reflected in the abundance of seafood dishes, while its history as a trading hub is evident in the liberal use of spices from India and Persia, like cardamom, saffron, and dried black lime (*loomi*). Sharing food is central to social life, and large communal platters are a symbol of hospitality and togetherness. The ubiquitous Bahraini breakfast of *balaleet* (sweet vermicelli with a saffron and cardamom omelet) is a perfect example of the fusion of flavors that defines the local palate.

In the space of two generations, Bahraini society has undergone a transformation of a scale and speed that is almost without historical precedent. A person born in a palm-frond *barasti* in the 1930s could live to see their grandchildren become global investment bankers working in glass skyscrapers built on land reclaimed from the sea. This rapid journey has created a society of contrasts: one that fiercely guards its traditions while embracing hyper-modernity, that values deep family ties while navigating the individualism of a globalized economy, and that contains a rich diversity of peoples while struggling with deep internal divisions. It is a society that continues to evolve, constantly recalibrating the delicate balance between its ancient island soul and its ambitious modern future.

CHAPTER TWENTY-THREE: The Changing Role of Women in Bahrain

In the Bahrain of the early 20th century, a woman's world was circumscribed by the walls of her home and the strictures of tradition. Society was organized around the rhythms of the sea and the date palm, and a woman's role within it was clear: to manage the household, raise children, and uphold the family's honor. Her life was largely private, her public visibility almost non-existent. The bustling, male-dominated worlds of the pearling dhow and the Manama souq were domains to which she had little access. The forces of modernity, however, were about to arrive, and they would be carried not on a merchant ship or by an oil prospector, but in the pages of a schoolbook. The story of the changing role of women in Bahrain is, above all, the story of education.

Even before the discovery of oil began to reshape the nation's economy, a quiet revolution was underway. In 1928, nine years after the first public school for boys was established, a group of progressive notables, with the encouragement of the state, opened the first formal school for girls. Originally named Al-Hidaya Al-Khalifiya for Girls, it was later renamed Khadija Al-Kubra School. At the time, the idea of formally educating girls was radical, a direct challenge to a deeply conservative social order that saw a woman's education as unnecessary at best and improper at worst. Yet the door had been opened, and it would never be closed again. The discovery of oil provided the fuel for this revolution to accelerate. A share of the new state revenues was plowed into creating a comprehensive public education system, and from the outset, schools for girls were an integral part of the plan.

This investment created a new social reality. A generation of Bahraini women grew up literate and numerate, their horizons expanded beyond the domestic sphere. With education came ambition. The initial forays into the workforce were tentative and confined to professions deemed socially acceptable for women, roles that were seen as extensions of their natural nurturing instincts. The first career paths to open up were in teaching and nursing. The government established the Higher Institute for Female Teachers in 1967 and the School of Nursing in 1959, creating formal pathways for women to enter these vital public service roles. They were pioneers, the first women to earn an independent salary and to navigate the complexities of a professional life outside the home.

As the state bureaucracy expanded and the private sector modernized, new opportunities began to emerge. Women started to take up clerical and administrative roles in government ministries and in the burgeoning banking sector. They proved to be skilled and reliable employees, gradually overcoming the skepticism of a male-dominated professional world. This economic empowerment had a profound, if gradual, effect on family life and social dynamics, giving women a new degree of personal autonomy and a voice in household decisions. To support this growing cohort of professional women, a network of civil society organizations began to form. Groups like the Children and Mothers Welfare Society and the Al Nahda (Awakening) Society provided charitable services but also served as the first platforms for women to organize, advocate, and engage in public life.

Despite these significant social and economic advances, the political arena remained a closed door. As Bahrain moved towards independence, women played a recognized role in the public sphere, with representatives from women's societies participating in the 1970 UN mission to ascertain the wishes of the people regarding their national identity. However, when the country's first constitution was drafted in 1973, it enshrined a glaring contradiction. While the document declared that all citizens were equal before the law, the electoral law that followed did not recognize women's suffrage. For the first national elections to the new parliament, the electorate was restricted to native-born male citizens. A petition presented by women's groups to the Amir requesting the right to vote was politely declined. For the next quarter-century, Bahraini women could become doctors, engineers, and entrepreneurs, but they could not cast a ballot or stand for office.

The dawn of the new millennium brought a dramatic reversal of fortune. The accession of King Hamad bin Isa Al Khalifa in 1999 ushered in an era of sweeping reform, and the empowerment of women was placed at the very center of his modernizing agenda. One of his first and most significant acts was the establishment of the Supreme Council for Women (SCW) in August 2001. Chaired by his wife, Her Royal Highness Princess Sabeeka bint Ibrahim Al Khalifa, the SCW was created as a powerful, high-level advisory body reporting directly to the King. Its mandate was to oversee all official efforts related to women's rights, propose legislation, and ensure that the principle of gender equality was integrated into all aspects of national development.

The National Action Charter of 2001, and the 2002 Constitution that followed, finally shattered the political glass ceiling. The new constitution was unequivocal, explicitly stating that "Citizens, both men and women, are entitled to participate in public affairs and may enjoy political rights, including the right to vote and to stand for elections". After decades of exclusion, Bahraini women had achieved full political equality on paper. The state actively encouraged women to participate in the first parliamentary and municipal elections of the new era in 2002. Several women stood as candidates, but in a field dominated by established male networks and boycotted by the main opposition groups, none were successful.

The government, however, was determined to ensure female representation. The King used his power of appointment to the upper chamber of parliament, the Shura Council, to place six women among its forty members, including one Christian and one Jewish woman. This became a consistent policy, guaranteeing a female presence at the heart of the legislative process. The real breakthrough came in April 2004, when Dr. Nada Haffadh was appointed Minister of Health, becoming Bahrain's first-ever female cabinet minister. The appointment was hailed as a historic moment, a clear signal that the highest levels of executive power were now open to women. This was followed by the appointment of the first female judges and ambassadors, steadily normalizing the presence of women in positions of authority.

The electoral breakthrough came in 2006. Lateefa Al Gaoud, a financial expert working in the Ministry of Finance, made history when she won a seat in the Council of Representatives by default after her opponents in the constituency withdrew. She was the first woman in Bahrain, and indeed in the Gulf, to be elected to a national parliament. In the years that followed, the number of women winning seats through the ballot box slowly grew, culminating in the 2018 election, when six women were elected to the lower house and one of them, Fawzia Zainal, was chosen by her peers to be the Speaker of the Council of Representatives, another first for the nation.

The tumultuous events of the 2011 uprising revealed the full extent of women's integration into the country's political life. Women were not passive observers; they were active participants on all sides of the conflict. They were highly visible in the protests at the Pearl Roundabout, marching, organizing, and speaking out. Figures like the activist Zainab al-Khawaja gained international prominence for their defiant acts of civil disobedience. Women also bore the brunt of the state's crackdown. They faced arrest, imprisonment, and torture, with female medics and teachers being particularly targeted for their perceived roles in the uprising. At the same time, other women were prominent defenders of the government, organizing pro-monarchy rallies and, in their official capacities, articulating the state's narrative. The conflict showed that Bahraini women were no longer confined to a single role, but were now fully engaged, and deeply divided, actors across the entire political spectrum.

Despite the remarkable progress in the political and professional spheres, a major battle for women's rights was being fought on a different front: the family. For decades, one of the most significant obstacles to full equality was the absence of a codified personal status law. Matters of marriage, divorce, child custody, and inheritance were adjudicated in separate religious courts for the Sunni and Shia communities. These courts were run exclusively by male judges, whose rulings were often based on their own interpretation of religious texts, leading to arbitrary and inconsistent judgments that overwhelmingly disadvantaged women.

For years, a coalition of women's rights activists waged a relentless campaign, demanding a single, unified civil family law that would protect women and children by providing clear, predictable legal standards. The campaign faced ferocious opposition from conservative religious circles, particularly from senior Shia clerics, who argued that only they had the authority to interpret religious law in these matters and that any civil law would be a violation of Islamic principles. The government, caught between the demands of the modernizers and the power of the clerics, moved cautiously.

A partial victory was achieved in 2009, when a personal status law covering only the Sunni community was passed. While this provided crucial protections for Sunni women, it left Shia women subject to the old system, creating a stark legal disparity within the female population. The campaign continued, and finally, after the political climate shifted in the wake of the uprising, the government pushed through a unified law. In July 2017, a new Family Law was passed that extended legal protections to both communities, a landmark achievement for the women's rights movement that had been decades in the making.

One significant legal hurdle remains. Bahrain's nationality law, which dates back to 1963, does not grant women the same rights as men to pass on their citizenship. While the children of a Bahraini father are automatically granted citizenship regardless of their mother's nationality, the children of a Bahraini mother and a foreign father are not. This has left thousands of children born to Bahraini women living in a state of legal limbo in their own country, often facing difficulties in accessing state services like education, healthcare, and employment. Activists continue to campaign for an amendment to the law, arguing that it is a clear violation of the constitutional principle of equality.

CHAPTER TWENTY-FOUR: Crafting the Future: Bahrain's Economic Vision 2030

By the mid-2000s, Bahrain was riding high on a wave of petrodollar-fueled prosperity. The reform project initiated by King Hamad had ushered in a period of political optimism, and a global oil boom was filling the state's coffers at an unprecedented rate. Cranes dotted the Manama skyline, land was being reclaimed from the sea for spectacular real estate projects, and the country's status as the financial hub of the Middle East seemed unassailable. Yet, beneath the shimmering surface of this boom, a familiar anxiety lingered. The country's leaders, more keenly aware than most of their modest hydrocarbon reserves, knew that this golden age was borrowed time. The oil would not last forever, and the state's paternalistic economic model, in which the government acted as the primary employer and driver of growth, was becoming unsustainable.

The core challenge was demographic. A young and rapidly growing population was entering the workforce, creating a demand for high-quality jobs that the public sector could no longer absorb. The private sector, while vibrant in pockets, was still heavily dependent on government spending and expatriate labor. For Bahrain to secure a prosperous future, it needed a fundamental shift in its economic DNA. It needed to move from an economy based on the extraction of wealth to one based on productivity and innovation. The old strategy of diversification, which had served the country well for three decades, needed a comprehensive, long-term blueprint for the 21st century.

This was the genesis of Bahrain's Economic Vision 2030. Launched in October 2008 with considerable fanfare, the Vision was not just another five-year plan. It was an aspirational, thirty-year roadmap intended to guide the nation's entire development trajectory. Its overarching goal was ambitious and elegantly simple: "to shift from an economy built on oil wealth to a productive, globally competitive economy, shaped by the government and driven by a pioneering private sector." The document was the culmination of four years of intensive consultation involving government bodies, private sector leaders, and international experts. It was a deliberate attempt to create a national consensus around a shared economic destiny.

The entire philosophy of the Vision was built on three core principles: Sustainability, Competitiveness, and Fairness. Sustainability was the headline act, the explicit goal of moving the economy away from its dependence on finite hydrocarbon resources and creating a more durable model. This meant not only fiscal sustainability for the government but also environmental sustainability, a nod to the growing global awareness of climate change and the unique ecological fragility of a small island nation.

Competitiveness was the engine designed to drive this transition. The plan recognized that in a globalized world, Bahrain could not compete on the scale of its neighbors, but it could compete on quality. This meant fostering a business environment that was a magnet for investment, with world-class infrastructure, a skilled workforce, and, crucially, a regulatory framework that was transparent, efficient, and fair. The goal was to make Bahrain one of the best places in the world to do business, a hub where productivity, not just connections, determined success.

Fairness was the social contract that underpinned the entire project. The architects of the Vision understood that a purely free-market approach could exacerbate social inequalities and undermine national unity. The principle of fairness was a promise that the benefits of future growth would be shared by all. It meant that every Bahraini should have the opportunity to prosper through their own hard work, with access to high-quality education, healthcare, and training. It also meant providing a social safety net for those who were unable to provide for themselves. This was a crucial element, a pledge that the transition to a more competitive, private sector-led economy would not leave the average citizen behind.

To translate these broad principles into concrete action, the Vision identified several key areas for strategic focus. Education was paramount. The plan called for a radical overhaul of the public education system, from primary school to university, to move away from rote memorization and towards critical thinking, problem-solving, and the skills demanded by the modern economy. Vocational training was to be revamped to create a pipeline of skilled Bahraini technicians for the country's growing industrial and service sectors.

Healthcare was another priority. The goal was to transform the existing system, which was almost entirely state-funded and provided, into a more diverse and efficient one, with a greater role for the private sector in providing services and a national health insurance scheme to manage costs. The aim was to create a system that was both higher in quality and more financially sustainable in the long term.

In the private sector, the Vision targeted several high-potential industries where Bahrain could build a competitive advantage. Finance was already a success story, and the plan called for deepening this expertise, particularly in high-growth areas like Islamic finance and financial technology (FinTech). Manufacturing, building on the success of the aluminium sector, was to be expanded. Logistics, leveraging Bahrain's strategic location at the heart of the Gulf, was identified as a key growth engine, with major investments planned for the country's port and airport. Finally, tourism and hospitality were to be developed, moving beyond the established regional market to attract a more international clientele.

To oversee this grand design, the government relied on the Economic Development Board (EDB), the powerful agency chaired by the Crown Prince, Sheikh Salman bin Hamad Al Khalifa. The EDB acted as the chief strategist and promoter of the Vision, its primary interface with the global investment community. To ensure the long-term vision was translated into concrete, medium-term steps, the government also launched a series of rolling National Economic Strategies. The first of these, for 2009-2014, laid out a detailed program of legal, regulatory, and institutional reforms needed to get the ball rolling. Key initiatives included a comprehensive reform of the labor market, designed to make hiring Bahrainis more attractive for private companies, and a major push to streamline the process of starting a business.

Just as this ambitious, carefully calibrated machine was beginning to turn, it was hit by two seismic shocks. The first was internal. The political uprising of 2011 and its tumultuous aftermath dealt a severe blow to the economic agenda. The immediate impact was a collapse in investor confidence and a sharp downturn in the tourism sector. The 2011 Formula 1 Grand Prix had to be cancelled, a decision that sent a powerful negative signal to the global community. More fundamentally, the crisis shifted the government's focus and resources. National security and domestic stability became the overriding priorities, and the state budget was increasingly directed towards security spending and social subsidies designed to quell discontent. The national consensus that the Vision had sought to build was shattered by the deep political and sectarian polarization.

The second shock was external. In mid-2014, global oil prices began a catastrophic slide, falling from over $100 a barrel to less than $30 by early 2016. For Bahrain, which still relied on oil and gas for over 70% of its state revenue, the crash was a fiscal disaster. The era of easy surpluses was over, replaced by yawning budget deficits. The government was forced into a period of painful austerity. Subsidies on fuel, electricity, and water were slashed, a move that was deeply unpopular and placed a new strain on household incomes. The financial firepower needed to fund the large-scale infrastructure and training projects at the heart of the Vision was severely depleted.

The confluence of these two crises—political turmoil followed by a fiscal crunch—forced a major recalibration of the Vision 2030 strategy. The aspirational goals remained, but the path to achieving them had to become more pragmatic and focused. Instead of relying on its own oil wealth, Bahrain now had to aggressively court foreign investment and rely on financial support from its wealthier Gulf neighbors. The $10 billion GCC development fund, pledged in 2011, became a crucial lifeline, funding major projects like the expansion and modernization of Bahrain International Airport, the construction of new public housing, and the development of the road network.

In this new, more constrained environment, the EDB's role became even more critical. The focus shifted to targeted reforms that cost little but could have a big impact on the business environment. The country embraced the digital economy with a new sense of urgency. A "cloud-first" policy was adopted, encouraging data to be hosted in Bahrain, and major global players like Amazon Web Services were attracted to set up their first regional data centers on the island. A regulatory sandbox was created by the Central Bank of Bahrain to allow FinTech startups to test new products and services in a live environment, a move that positioned Bahrain as a leading hub for financial innovation in the region.

New sectors were prioritized. Recognizing the potential of its strategic location and the new, state-of-the-art Khalifa Bin Salman Port, a major push was made to develop the logistics and e-commerce sectors. A new Bahrain Logistics Zone was established, offering streamlined services and customs procedures to attract international companies looking for a regional distribution hub.

By the early 2020s, the results of this long and often difficult journey were clear to see. The structure of the Bahraini economy had been fundamentally altered. The contribution of the non-oil sector to the country's GDP had risen steadily, accounting for over 80% of the total, a clear sign of successful diversification. The financial services sector had overtaken oil as the single largest contributor to the economy. The modernized airport, opened in 2021, was a world-class gateway to the island, and the new real estate developments had transformed the nation's urban profile. In 2021, the government launched a new Economic Recovery Plan, a package of reforms and investments designed to boost post-COVID growth and accelerate the Vision's goals, with a particular focus on attracting over $30 billion in new investments by 2023.

This plan prioritized six key sectors: oil and gas, tourism, logistics, financial services, telecommunications and IT, and manufacturing.

Despite these tangible successes, the core challenges that the Vision was designed to address remained. Government debt had soared as a result of the years of low oil prices and high spending, reaching over 100% of GDP. The creation of high-wage jobs for Bahrainis in the private sector continued to be a struggle, and youth unemployment remained a persistent social and political concern. The principle of Fairness, the third pillar of the Vision, proved the most difficult to achieve in a climate of political division and fiscal austerity. The grand project of crafting the future, launched in a moment of supreme confidence, had been battered and reshaped by the unpredictable storms of the subsequent decade. The journey was far from over, but the map, first drawn in 2008, was still the one being used to navigate the uncertain road ahead.

CHAPTER TWENTY-FIVE:
Contemporary Challenges and the Road Ahead

To look at Bahrain in the third decade of the 21st century is to witness a nation caught between the powerful inertia of its history and the relentless demands of the future. The grand projects of the past half-century—the creation of a modern state, the diversification of the economy, the careful navigation of a perilous region—have been largely successful. The skyline of Manama, a thicket of glass towers rising from reclaimed land, stands as a gleaming testament to that success. Yet, the road ahead is shadowed by a series of profound and interconnected challenges that will test the kingdom's renowned resilience in new and demanding ways. The political questions left unanswered by the tumult of 2011, the precariousness of a state budget still yoked to the price of oil, and the complexities of a shifting global order have created a daunting policy landscape for the nation's leadership.

The most immediate and sensitive of these challenges is the unresolved political question. The decade following the 2011 uprising was one of comprehensive consolidation by the state. The organized political opposition, both religious and secular, was systematically dismantled, its leaders imprisoned and its societies dissolved. The result is a political landscape of enforced quiescence. Elections for the lower house of parliament are held, but they are neither free nor fully competitive, with "political isolation laws" barring former members of opposition parties from participating. The chamber they produce is largely composed of pro-government independents, a body that can debate local issues but lacks the power or the cohesion to act as a meaningful check on the executive. For the government, this state of affairs represents the restoration of stability and the defeat of a sectarian threat. For a significant portion of the population, however, it represents the hollowing out of the democratic promise of the National Action Charter.

This political stalemate presents a long-term structural risk. In the absence of legitimate channels for dissent, grievances fester beneath the surface. While mass street protests are a distant memory, the conditions in the country's prisons remain a point of friction. In August 2023, a hunger strike involving over 800 inmates at Jau Prison, many of them held since 2011, drew international attention to their demands for better conditions and adequate healthcare. In a significant move in 2024, King Hamad granted a series of mass pardons, releasing thousands of prisoners, including a substantial number of those detained for political reasons. The move was widely welcomed as a step toward easing tensions. Yet, key opposition and human rights leaders, including figures like Abdulhadi al-Khawaja and Hassan Mushaima, remain behind bars, and human rights organizations continue to criticize what they describe as an environment of repression. The road ahead requires a delicate search for a new, more inclusive political consensus, one that can bridge the deep divides left by the last decade without, in the government's view, compromising the stability of the state.

This political challenge is inextricably linked to an equally pressing economic one. For years, Bahrain's economic model was a straightforward social contract: the state, enriched by oil revenues, provided its citizens with cradle-to-grave welfare, including subsidized goods and services and ample public sector employment, in return for political loyalty. The collapse of oil prices in 2014 shattered the financial foundations of this arrangement. The era of easy surpluses vanished, replaced by a string of deep budget deficits. Government debt, a minor concern in the boom years, ballooned to alarming levels, exceeding 120% of GDP.

The state was forced to embark on a painful but necessary path of fiscal reform. A Fiscal Balance Program, first introduced in 2018 and updated after the COVID-19 pandemic, sought to rein in the deficit. Subsidies on fuel, electricity, and water were cut. New revenue streams were sought, most notably through the introduction of a Value Added Tax (VAT) in 2019, a move once unthinkable in the tax-free Gulf. These measures were taken under the watchful eye of Bahrain's wealthier neighbors. A $10 billion financial support package from Saudi Arabia, the UAE, and Kuwait in 2018 was a crucial lifeline, preventing a full-blown debt crisis but also underscoring the kingdom's economic vulnerability. The target of balancing the budget has been repeatedly pushed back, and the fiscal squeeze remains the government's single greatest economic challenge. Every policy decision must now be weighed on a fiscal tightrope: how to cut spending and raise revenue without placing an unbearable burden on a populace long accustomed to state largesse.

This fiscal pressure complicates another, even more fundamental, challenge: creating enough high-quality jobs for a young and growing population. For decades, the government was the employer of first resort for most Bahrainis. The Vision 2030 strategy explicitly seeks to shift this dynamic, making the private sector the primary engine of job creation. However, the reality has been difficult. Youth unemployment, while lower than in some parts of the wider Middle East, remains stubbornly high. A core issue is the structure of the labor market, in which a large private sector workforce of low-wage expatriates creates intense competition for entry-level positions. The government's "Bahrainization" policies and initiatives, such as the National Labour Market Plan, aim to make hiring Bahrainis more attractive for private companies, with ambitious annual targets for employment and training. The long-term success of the kingdom will depend heavily on its ability to win this race, to produce skilled graduates and to foster a private sector dynamic enough to absorb them into productive, well-paying careers.

While grappling with these internal pressures, Bahrain must also navigate an increasingly complex and competitive regional environment. The strategic alignment with Saudi Arabia remains the cornerstone of its foreign policy, a non-negotiable guarantee of its security. However, Saudi Arabia's own transformative Vision 2030, with its goal of becoming a global hub for business and tourism, presents a new competitive challenge. For years, Bahrain benefited from being the more liberal and accessible destination on Saudi Arabia's doorstep. As Saudi Arabia opens up socially and aggressively courts foreign investment, Bahrain must work harder to define and defend its own unique value proposition.

The relationship with Iran remains the primary security preoccupation. The Saudi-Iranian rapprochement, brokered by China in 2023, created a new diplomatic reality. Following Riyadh's lead, Bahrain began its own talks with Tehran in mid-2024 to discuss the restoration of diplomatic ties, which had been severed in 2016. This move represents a shift from confrontation to cautious diplomacy, but the underlying strategic rivalry and deep-seated suspicion remain.

The Abraham Accords of 2020, which saw Bahrain normalize relations with Israel, was a landmark strategic realignment. Driven by a shared perception of the threat from Iran, the accord promised a new era of security and economic cooperation. While the relationship was deepened with the exchange of ambassadors and the signing of various agreements, the subsequent war in Gaza put the public-facing aspects of the relationship on hold, highlighting the domestic sensitivity of the issue. Nonetheless, the underlying strategic logic of the alliance remains a key feature of Bahrain's contemporary foreign policy.

Beyond the immediate region, the great power competition between the United States and China presents both opportunities and dilemmas. The U.S. remains the indispensable security partner, the ultimate guarantor of regional stability and the protector of the sea lanes upon which Bahrain's economy depends. At the same time, China has become a crucial economic partner, the largest source of imports and a key potential investor. The road ahead requires a deft diplomatic touch, maintaining the vital security alliance with Washington while simultaneously cultivating the growing economic relationship with Beijing.

Looming over all these challenges is the inexorable reality of climate change. As a low-lying desert archipelago with scarce water resources, Bahrain is exceptionally vulnerable to rising sea levels and extreme heat. This has prompted the government to begin its own energy transition. The National Energy Transition Plan outlines targets to increase the share of renewable energy in the power generation mix to 20% by 2035 and to achieve net-zero emissions by 2060. These are ambitious goals for a state whose economy was built on fossil fuels. The main obstacle is a simple lack of space for large-scale solar or wind farms. The government is therefore exploring creative solutions, from installing solar panels on the rooftops of government buildings to exploring the potential for offshore wind. The success of this transition is not just an environmental issue; it is a core component of the country's long-term economic sustainability.

In the face of these hurdles, the kingdom has staked much of its future on becoming a pioneer in the digital economy. It has aggressively courted investment in financial technology, creating progressive regulatory frameworks for everything from open banking to crypto assets. The government's own "cloud-first" policy and the establishment of major data centers by global tech giants are part of a concerted strategy to position Bahrain as a key digital hub for the region. This technological ambition represents one of the brightest paths forward, a way to leverage the country's skilled, youthful population and its reputation for sound regulation.

The history of Bahrain has been a story of constant adaptation. From the Bronze Age traders of Dilmun to the pearl merchants of the 19th century and the bankers of the 21st, its people have always found a way to turn their small island's strategic location into an advantage. The challenges of today—of political reconciliation, fiscal sustainability, and regional security—are as formidable as any the nation has faced. The road ahead is uncertain, its contours shaped by forces both local and global. Crafting a prosperous and stable future will require all the pragmatism, resilience, and adaptability that have defined the island's long and remarkable journey.

AFTERWORD

To reach the end of a story that spans five millennia is to be left with a profound sense of both change and continuity. When I began this project, I was drawn to the paradox of the island, that peculiar geography of connection and isolation that the Introduction sought to outline. Having now traced the long arc of Bahrain's history, from the first cuneiform whispers of Dilmun to the digital hum of Manama's financial district, that paradox feels more acute and more essential than ever. Bahrain's story is not a simple, linear progression; it is a spiral, constantly circling back to familiar themes—of trade, of foreign influence, of internal identity—but at a different elevation, in a new context.

What has struck me most forcefully in the course of this research is the sheer resilience of the island's core identity as a crossroads. This is not a place that has ever had the luxury of isolation. Its destiny, from its earliest days as a Bronze Age entrepôt linking Mesopotamia and the Indus Valley, has been to be a node in a network, a meeting point. The names have changed—Dilmun, Tylos, Mishmahig, Bahrain—and the masters have come and gone—Sumerians, Greeks, Persians, Portuguese, British—but the fundamental character of the place has endured. It has always been a space of transaction, not just of goods like copper, pearls, and oil, but of ideas, cultures, and faiths. This constant exposure to the outside world could have erased its local character, yet it has instead forged a unique and remarkably adaptable identity, one that has learned to absorb, appropriate, and Bahrainize foreign influences without being subsumed by them. The Hellenistic gravestones of Tylos, with their distinct fusion of Greek style and Semitic features, feel like an early metaphor for a process that has never stopped.

The second recurring pattern is that of the resource lottery, the cycle of boom and bust that has so often defined the islands' fortunes. For centuries, Bahrain's fate was tied to the iridescent whim of the oyster. The pearl trade built a complex society and fabulous wealth, but its collapse in the 1930s was a near-death experience for the nation. It was a stark lesson in the precarity of a single-product economy. Then, at the moment of greatest desperation, the lottery was won again, this time with the discovery of oil. This second boom was an order of magnitude more transformative than the first, funding the creation of a modern state and a welfare system that remade the life of every citizen.

Yet, as this history has shown, Bahrain's leaders seem to have internalized the lesson of the pearls. The knowledge that the oil, too, is a finite gift has instilled a unique sense of urgency in their long-term planning. The conscious, decades-long effort to build an economy "beyond the oil fields" is perhaps the defining project of modern Bahrain. The pivot to heavy industry, then to offshore finance, and now to technology and logistics is a remarkable story of strategic foresight. It is an attempt to finally break the cycle, to build a future based not on what can be extracted from the earth or the sea, but on what can be created by the minds and skills of its people.

Finally, there is the most complex and sensitive thread running through this modern history: the quest for a stable and inclusive political settlement. The journey from a traditional sheikhdom to a British protectorate, and from an independent state to a constitutional monarchy, has been fraught with tension. The memory of the 1973 parliament, the trauma of the 1990s uprising, the soaring hopes and bitter disappointments of the National Action Charter, and the profound schism of 2011 are not just historical events; they are living legacies that continue to shape the present.

Writing the recent chapters of this book was a delicate task, a reminder that history is not a settled, dusty affair but a contested and often painful narrative, particularly for those who have lived it. The events of 2011, in particular, left deep wounds that have yet to fully heal, hardening identities and damaging the social trust that had been a quiet strength of Bahraini society. The great challenge for the nation, as it looks ahead, is to reconcile the imperatives of state security with the legitimate aspirations for political participation that have surfaced repeatedly throughout its modern history.

To write a history of Bahrain is, in the end, to tell the story of a survivor. It has survived the decline of ancient empires and the collapse of its own economies. It has weathered foreign invasion, regional wars, and profound internal conflict. Its long history does not offer simple predictions for its future, but it does reveal a deep reservoir of pragmatism and an extraordinary capacity for adaptation. The island of the two seas has always been a place of confluence, where fresh water meets salt, where East meets West, and where tradition meets modernity. The story written here is but one telling of that long, complex, and unfinished journey.

Printed in Dunstable, United Kingdom

77649745R00087

Digital Transformation in Financial Services